THE GATHER...

For my mum, for your conviction and your passion, for your profound sense of social justice. You wouldn't have walked a pilgrimage, but I know you would have approved.

THE GATHERING PLACE

*A Winter Pilgrimage Through
Changing Times*

Mary Colwell

BLOOMSBURY WILDLIFE
LONDON · OXFORD · NEW YORK · NEW DELHI · SYDNEY

BLOOMSBURY WILDLIFE
Bloomsbury Publishing Plc
50 Bedford Square, London, WC1B 3DP, UK
29 Earlsfort Terrace, Dublin 2, Ireland

BLOOMSBURY, BLOOMSBURY WILDLIFE and the Diana logo are trademarks
of Bloomsbury Publishing Plc

First published in the United Kingdom 2023

A catalogue record for this book is available from the British Library

Library of Congress Cataloguing-in-Publication data has been applied for

ISBN: 978-1-3994-0054-1; Audio download: 978-1-3994-0053-4;
ePDF: 978-1-3994-0057-2; ePub: 978-1-3994-0055-8

2 4 6 8 10 9 7 5 3 1

Typeset in Bembo Std by Deanta Global Publishing Services, Chennai, India
Printed and bound in Great Britain by CPI Group (UK) Ltd., Croydon, CR0 4YY

MIX
Paper | Supporting
responsible forestry
FSC® C171272

To find out more about our authors and books visit www.bloomsbury.com
and sign up for our newsletters

Contents

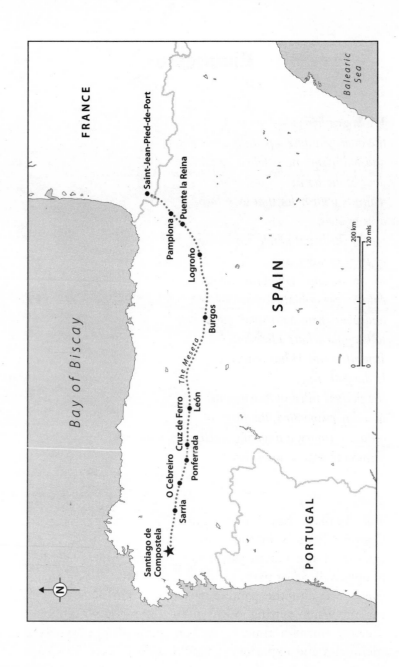

FRANCE

SPAIN

PORTUGAL

Bay of Biscay

Balearic Sea

Saint-Jean-Pied-de-Port

Pamplona

Puente la Reina

Logroño

Burgos

The Meseta

León

Cruz de Ferro

Ponferrada

O Cebreiro

Sarria

Santiago de Compostela

N

200 km

120 mls

Prologue

We are gatherers,
the ones who pick up sticks and stones
and old wasp's nests fallen by the
door of the barn,
walnuts with holes that look like
eyes of owls,
bits of shells not whole but lovely
in their brokenness,
we are the ones who bring home
empty eggs of birds
and place them on a small glass shelf
to keep for what? How long?
It matters not. What matters
is the gathering,
the pockets filled with remnants
of a day evaporated, the traces of
certain memory, a lingering smell,
a smile that came with the shell.

Nina Bagley, 'Gathering'

This book is based on a gathering journey along the Camino Francés in the autumn/winter of 2020, in the middle of the Covid pandemic. Normally, over 300,000 people walk all or part of this ancient, 500-mile pilgrimage every year, but the pandemic meant I had most of it to myself. When setting out I didn't know it would be a journey through time as well as space, that unexpected memories and experiences would surface to sit alongside the more usual spiritual quest. Gatherings coalesce on this ancient pathway of longing and endeavour, and time and distance help sift and sort what has meaning.

My pilgrimage began when the world was in a different place than at the time of writing this prologue, at the very end of 2022. In the autumn of 2020, Donald Trump was still president of the United States of America, the UK had not seceded from Europe and Boris Johnson was still in power. The war in Ukraine had not begun and there were no energy or cost of living crises. We were just entering the stormy waters that would see unprecedented changes in government, world order and environmental emergencies – global events we are in the middle of today. It was a pilgrimage undertaken at a time when the foundations upon which we all stand were beginning to quake. Everything was uncertain, nothing felt normal. Packing a bag and walking a pilgrimage was my response to changing times.

The first lockdown had ended in early summer of 2020 and Britain was tentatively venturing outside. The UK government advised against travel, but it was permitted under restricted circumstances if testing, masks and distancing were obeyed. Vaccines were not yet available, although a breakthrough was tantalisingly close and would become a reality by the end of the year.

In some ways, it was a strange decision, to walk alone across northern Spain when there was so much uncertainty, but then pilgrims have always taken to the road in times of turmoil, through wars, plagues and upheaval; and there is nothing this ancient trackway hasn't seen before. Walking a sacred trail through turbulent times is one way to connect the past to the present, to hitch an anxious soul to the countless millions of others who have tried to make sense of chaos, to understand more about being human on a challenging planet.

The Camino Francés, often referred to as simply the Camino, is one of the oldest Christian pilgrimages in the world, following even older trade routes over the Pyrenees and across northern Spain, and ending at the cathedral in Santiago de Compostela. It is an iconic journey with paradox at its heart. It is unchanged yet forever changing, old yet always new. Although the route stays the same, it holds as many different meanings for people as there are stars in the sky, echoing an alternative name, the Path of the Milky Way.

Pilgrimage of all kinds is growing in popularity, exponentially so in some parts of the world. People are searching for meaning and affirmation as life becomes ever more alienating. Taking one step at a time is as ancient as humanity itself, and walking with purpose to a special destination adds a layer that is invaluable.

The Gathering Place is not a guide to the Camino, there are many fine travel books which give all the practical advice you could ever need. I have simply documented my own experience of walking across Spain in the middle of a pandemic when the land was empty of people, and it turned out to be far more than I ever expected.

The usual greeting given to and between pilgrims on the Camino is 'Buen Camino' – good journey. It is a recognition that something is happening that is different to a normal hike. I heard it nearly every day. At the end, as I stood outside the cathedral of St James in Santiago de Compostela, I posted a tweet, 'Whatever journey you find yourself on, I sincerely wish you Buen Camino.' Wherever you are, no matter what place you find yourself in, emotionally, spiritually, physically, have a good onward journey in every sense of the word. I hope you face whatever comes your way with a good heart and a calm soul.

CHAPTER ONE

Wooden Staffs and Mountains

Propped up against the entrance to a café in a small mountain village is a *very* long staff, it must be over two metres tall. The smooth, caramel-coloured wood was once a branch of a tree, maybe even a sapling, but it has been carefully stripped and polished into an oversized walking stick. It is a simple and lovely thing that looks at ease against the stone wall, as though it is used to waiting. I study the outside tables for the owner, but no one looks like a walker, and certainly nobody is tall enough to use such a long stick. They seem to be locals enjoying a socially-distanced coffee with friends in the weak October sunshine, and they nod at me as I sit down, resting my rucksack and two metal walking poles next to the table. Throughout breakfast I can't help staring at the staff and wondering who would carry it, and why.

Trees don't travel unless we take them with us. Our earliest ancestors would have used them as weapons as well as aids, and we continue that practice, as though fashioning sticks is part of our DNA. But there is more to it than that; a wooden staff possesses characteristics that makes it a good companion as well as a useful tool. Once chopped down and taken away from its earthy roots, a wooden pole quickly transforms into a treasured possession in ways that a mass-produced metal one does not. Hewn with sensitivity, a staff retains some of the character and stoicism of its parent tree. Some become works of art, with decorations and intricate carvings, which shifts them further into the human realm. Our complex lives are written into their grain and texture;

they become representative of and integral to who we think we are. Curly-topped croziers are used by shepherds and bishops to gather their flocks, masons' rods are topped with gold and silver emblems, heavy-topped canes were once wielded by bailiffs, city gents encrusted their walking sticks with mother-of-pearl, silver and jewels and weary peasants leant on their bare supports along life's rough road. There are many ways to relate to a wooden staff, many shades of weight, quality and colour, but this one outside a café on a mountain road is most definitely someone's friend.

I wonder if it belongs to a giant. Why not? Even giants must have dreams, big seven-league-boot-sized dreams that spur them to set forth on a journey. Any stories I have ever read about giants have them striding around the world, taking no time to cross whole countries and even seas – and maybe this giant has a pilgrim's heart. The café, after all, is on the famous pilgrimage trail known as the Camino Francés, The Way of St James, often shortened to The Way, or simply the Camino.

Granted World Heritage Site status in 1993, it is a renowned, 500-mile pathway that starts in the foothills of the French Pyrenees and ends in the far west of Spain at the Catedral de Santiago de Compostela. This grand destination is believed to be the final resting place of the bones of a Roman-era fisherman and friend of Jesus of Nazareth, St James. Christian tradition has it that in AD 44, his martyred remains were brought here from Jerusalem, where he had been beheaded on the order of Herod Agrippa I. James had been the first to evangelize on the Iberian Peninsula before returning to the Middle East and to his martyrdom. The location of the tomb was lost from memory until, in the ninth century, a shepherd called Pelayo is said to have rediscovered it. He followed a shower of stars into a field, giving the site the poetic name of Santiago de Compostela, or St James of the Starry Meadow. From that time onwards, people were drawn to pay homage from all parts of the Christian world, making use of existing trade routes that ferried goods to and from the shoulder of Spain. To entice more seekers of God, ever-grander buildings were erected on the burial site and along the main routes to it, and the roads and footpaths serviced to provide food, accommodation and medicine for travellers. It became self-mythologising and hugely popular. At its medieval peak, hundreds of thousands of people walked the Camino each year, but it was not to last. Pilgrimage to Santiago experienced centuries of abandonment, falling out of favour from the sixteenth century due to the Reformation, wars and plagues. It was not until the end of the twentieth century that it was reimagined and reinvigorated for a more modern mindset. Today, walking the Camino is going from strength to strength. Despite a move away from traditional religion, there is still a pilgrim impulse inside many of us.

Like so many relics around the world, the bones of St James have become monumental and symbolic; magnets that draw people to connect the spirit world with that of the living through a physical reminder of our own mortality. Under the weight of so much belief, legend and myth, bones transcend their physical reality to become a conduit to God. The facts about them become less important than the desire for a focus for spiritual expression.

Relics of saints became big business in medieval times, not only their whole bodies but fragments of bones and other body parts. Their inherent holiness was deemed capable of dispensing both healing and hope to those who sincerely sought them out, and soon relics were spread around Europe. The more prestigious the saint, the more widely distributed their relics, and consequently the more people would visit the site. A burgeoning trade in forgeries of saints' heads, arms, fingers, fingernails, tongues, dried blood and items of clothing developed, as well as a flourishing of skulduggery as relics were stolen and spirited away to other places. As Mary and Jesus are believed to have left no bodily remains, their relics, which were the most revered of all, took the form of breast milk, the umbilical cord, the foreskin of the circumcised baby Jesus and parts of the manger or cross. Even 'contact relics' of Jesus became important, pieces of earth where he was supposed to have stood, fragments of stone from his tomb, items of clothing, including the famous Turin Shroud, the cloth that was claimed to have been Jesus' burial shroud (which has since been proved to have been created between 1260 and 1390). To modern sensibilities these are strange and macabre obsessions, but before our rational, scientific age they promised physical access to holiness, something that was important to the medieval mind where the boundary between the physical planet, human flesh, the mind and the spirit world was fluid and complex.

A reconstruction of St James, based on an inventory of his alleged mortal remains, would produce an odd specimen of humanity. In an online forum on the Camino, a seasoned pilgrim carried out some research and found that St James had:

Three bodies in France (an authentic relic in Toulouse), and one in Spain (Santiago), nine heads in France and numerous limbs. One head in Jerusalem (it's still there in the Church of St James the Less). Five heads in Italy (two in Venice, one in Valencia, one in Amalfi, one in Artois). In the Church of the Apostles in Rome are preserved a piece of his skull and some of his blood.

There are bones, hands, and arms in Sicily, on the island of Capri, at Pavia, in Bavaria, at Liège and Cologne and a finger in Segovia and in Burgos. There was an arm preserved in Torcello near Venice from about the sixth century which was passed down to Henry V. His widow Matilda took the left hand to England where it became the prime relic at Reading Abbey and wrought many miracles. The abbey was destroyed by Henry VIII in 1538 during the dissolution of the monasteries and the relic disappeared. (In 1786 workmen digging at Reading Abbey found an old iron chest that contained a mummified hand believed by some to be the relic of Saint James. It now resides in a glass case at St Peter's Church, Marlow.) Altogether, from the sixth century, there were four bodies, fifteen heads, two places with parts of the skull, numerous limbs and finger bones.

Waggish comments accompany this posting, along the lines of people spreading themselves too thinly, but the humour is interspersed with serious considerations, which point out that the authenticity of the bones is of less interest than the meanings with which we imbue these dusty, fragile remains. Between the physical relics and the yearnings of the soul is built a citadel of tradition and history that has taken generations to construct, and it is not dismantled lightly. Even today, for some, just a glimpse of presumed physical holiness is a connection to eternity, a link between the fragile, fleeting human condition and the realm of the divine. Relics are still motivation enough for some to take to the road.

The destination of a pilgrimage is important, but so too is the journey to get there; they cannot be separated. A measure of travel and endeavour is vital, even if a flight or a car ride makes up the bulk of the distance. The time spent in expectation of arrival is not dead time, it is filled with thoughtfulness. Pilgrimage is defined by both the journey and the destination, and for many modern pilgrims on the Camino Francés, the journey is perhaps more important than the bones in the cathedral at Santiago itself.

This café breakfast on my first day of walking is a couple of hours away from one of the most popular starting points, the walled, medieval village of St-Jean-Pied-de-Port (St John at the foot of the pass) in southern France. Compact and enticing streets tumble down to bridges that span the River Nive. Everything a pilgrim could ever want is here: an office to collect a 'passport' for stamps as proof of the journey, information, maps, lists of lodgings, food, trinkets, guides, clothing, advice … it has been a gathering place for the start of an adventure for centuries.

In the 2010 film *The Way*, Dr Tom Avery (played by Martin Sheen), is angry that his son Daniel (played by Sheen's own son, Emilio Estevez) has given up a PhD at Berkeley to travel the world. Daniel longs to break away from the staid future he sees waiting for him; one of wealth, stability, conformity and safe pleasures like golf – a life led by his father. The prospect of a treadmill of boredom is wearying to Daniel's soul. As Tom sulkily drives him to the airport, they snap at each other. Hurt by rejection, Tom says that his lifestyle may not mean much to Daniel, but it is the life he chooses. Daniel retorts that you don't choose a life, you live one. It is a stinging criticism that hits home, and it proves to be their last exchange. Tragedy strikes when Daniel dies in bad weather crossing the Pyrenees and Tom travels to St-Jean-Pied-de-Port to identify his body. Driven by grief and a desire to understand why Daniel wanted to go on a pilgrimage, he packs his ashes into the rucksack and sets off on the Camino to complete what Daniel had started. It becomes a personal journey of redemption and healing; a story of relationships transformed, of loss, grief, acceptance, friendship, community, self-discovery and humility. The film was successful, and it sparked a Camino revival.

The winding road out of St-Jean-Pied-de-Port, exiting through the stone arch of the Porte d'Espagne (door of Spain), leads to the mountains and across the unmarked border between France and Spain. 'Mountains' is perhaps a stretch of the imagination; some prefer to call them 'cow hills'. They are at the western, petering-out end of the Pyrenees range; the highest peaks lie in the central area some 150 miles away, but as the walking is uphill and tiring, mountains is a fair description to me. In normal times, the small villages that scatter along the road offer a string of services for pilgrims, but these are not normal times. All the other cafés I have passed were shut and fellow travellers are few; I haven't seen another pilgrim since setting out at dawn. No doubt the approaching winter has a part to play, but more significantly, the virus that is raging around the world is putting humanity on high alert and keeping people indoors. And Covid is just one of a number of global events that are combining to make 2020 a strange, frightening, significant year. A pandemic, political upheavals at home and abroad, the increasing effects of climate change and the shocking decline of wildlife across the planet are shaking the foundations upon which we stand and which we have assumed were solid. Years of misuse of nature and each other sees chickens coming home to roost all over the earth.

The Covid crisis is manifest in this tiny mountain village through enforced social distancing and mandatory face masks; even the village statue sports one as a humorous reminder that this is no joke. One of the results of so

much worry is a Camino of empty streets and hostels.
The photographs in guidebooks which show hundreds of
pilgrims stretching into the distance haven't materialised,
and nor will they. My 2020 solo trek is destined to have
few fellow travellers. It seems, though, that I do have a
secretive giant for a companion.

Sitting at the foot of the long staff, like a faithful dog,
is a small, half-full rucksack. The two go together, they
are a duo. Both have that worn, loved look of belonging
to someone who is used to travelling swift and light. I
am impressed and envious. My rucksack is twice the
size and very heavy, way too heavy. Only a few hours in
and I know I will have to offload, but I can't imagine
having as little to rely on as this mystery traveller.
Traditional images have the medieval pilgrim walking
in sandals with just a small shoulder bag, a hollowed-
out gourd for carrying water, a wooden staff, a hat for
protection against the sun and a cloak, which can double
as a blanket. Few westerners in the twenty-first century
are this stoic or hardy enough to survive an arduous
journey on simplicity and prayer, I know I'm not. As a
tiny post office is just opening across the street, into a
box destined for home go binoculars, extra clothes and
thermals, some toiletries and a book. At the last moment
I think better of including my waterproof trousers. The
postmaster looks at the heavy package addressed to
Bristol as though I was asking for it to be sent to the
moon. Mountains of paperwork, a flurry of stamping,
gesticulations and whistling through teeth eventually
see me emerge 20 minutes later with a lighter wallet
and a more manageable pack, but in the meantime the
long staff and the small bag have gone. The giant has
quietly slipped away as only the mythical can, but in the

way of the Camino I have a feeling we will meet again
before we reach the cathedral in Santiago.

The Camino Francés is one of many Caminos that end
at the cathedral of St James, a complex web of trails that
wind across Great Britain and Europe which converge at
the tomb of precious bones. Thousands upon millions of
footsteps have made – and still make – their way to this
grand shrine. The Camino Norte traverses the northern
coast of northern Spain, the Camino Portuguese refers to
a number of routes that make their way through Portugal,
the Jacobswegs (St James' Ways) criss-cross Germany, the
Camino Ingles has pilgrims heading out from various
holy sites in England to the coast and then sailing to
north-west Spain. Other starting points range across
Europe, beginning at significant shrines, churches or
cathedrals, and ending at the same place. Some are over a
thousand miles in length, others just a few days' walk.
These channels of prayers and dreams grow in size and
strength as they near their destination, combining into a
torrent of souls for the last miles into Santiago. All these
pilgrimages are gathering places, drawing people to walk
the same ancient pathways through the modern world.

The various Caminos are a subset of many other
pilgrimage routes, threads of intention that spin a web of
spirituality across the physical world. Pathways both long
and short lead pilgrims of all kinds between innumerable
sites of significance, be they standing stones, ancient trees,
significant mountains, pre-Christian tombs, places of
worship, holy relics or sites of natural beauty. Pilgrimage
destinations need not be old or religious, they can
venerate the secular and the contemporary, but they must
be places that hold meaning. Literally millions of pilgrims

make countless journeys of various lengths for more
reasons than it is possible to list – and the numbers grow
year on year.

In 1985, 690 pilgrims were recorded on the Camino
Francés; by 2019, before the pandemic, it was almost
350,000, and only a small percentage of people defined
their motivation as purely religious. Even those routes
that have their foundations deep in traditional religions
are changing in the modern age. Magazines and
newspapers carry articles highlighting pilgrimage as the
post-Covid travel trend. Iain Tweedale, who leads guided
Camino walks, believes the increase in pilgrim numbers is
an expression of a desire to slow down and re-encounter
an older rhythm, which has been lost in modern times:
'After several days walking, when the mind calms, you
observe your surroundings more keenly, seeing simple
things like rocks, flowers and birds as if for the first time.
The outer journey from place to place becomes an inner
journey from head to heart … Covid has forced us to
stop, think, and question life's assumptions.' A quarter of
the way through the twenty-first century, it seems many
people are exhausted. Cracks are appearing, souls are
running on empty, people are searching for connection
and meaning. Modern-day pilgrimage is one way to
explore a more spiritual side of life without necessarily
being religious. The growth of pilgrimage of all kinds in
recent years is testament to the desire to re-enchant a
world dulled by human misuses and excesses.

Over the years I have undertaken a number of long
walks, but not many of them I would call pilgrimages,
they were adventures and holidays; pilgrimage came later.
In 2016 and 2017, I walked two secular pilgrimages and
would walk a further, more traditional one in Italy in
2021, the St Francis Way.

The 2016 walk was a 500-mile odyssey for an endangered bird called the Eurasian curlew. It started in the west of Ireland and finished on the east coast of England on the Wash. It was not a known route, no one had walked it before as far as I knew; the parameters had all been set by the bird. This was a journey through the life of curlews across the United Kingdom, defined by their nesting and wintering grounds and by the people who are working to save them. I went to places where they still sing, to the empty meadows that no longer resound to their beautiful calls, and to visit projects that are trying to bring them back from the brink. I met scientists, birdwatchers, poets, artists, conservationists and farmers – anyone who would talk to me about what the bird meant to them. The journey began in April in the meadows and moors where the birds breed, and ended where, come winter, thousands gather on the coast to see out the harshest months of the year. I called it the Curlew Walk, and my book, *Curlew Moon*, was the result.

The second secular pilgrimage was an established long-distance path through the Sierra Nevada mountains in California, the John Muir Trail (JMT). Thousands walk the 230-mile traverse of a high mountain range every year, most as a hiking challenge through spectacular terrain. In all, it climbs a total of over 4,400m. My motivation was not so much for the physical challenge, but to get closer to the spirit of my hero, the nineteenth-century environmentalist and naturalist, John Muir. Born in Scotland in 1838, his family moved to America when he was 11 years old to be frontier farmers and to live in a strict religious community. The tension between the wild wonder of a nature-rich America and the suffocation of his family's faith produced a white heat of creativity in Muir, and he grew up to change the heart of a nation.

Everywhere, magnificent landscapes were being deforested, mined, overfished, hunted out and transformed by growing industries that relied on natural resources. Through words so powerful that he ignited America's soul, he helped establish the world's first National Parks. I love Muir's writing, his kind and indomitable spirit, his open-hearted, vulnerable masculinity, his love of both people and wildness. In an era when Victorian frontiersmen were uncompromising, he bared his soul. When viewing the Californian mountains, Muir was so moved by the beauty before him, he wept. His stolid male colleague was nonplussed and stated he did not believe it was right to wear one's heart on one's sleeve. Slipping back into Scots dialect, as he did when emotional, Muir's response was, 'Ah, my dear mon, in the face of such a scene as this, it's no time to be thinkin' o' where to wear your heart.' This is why I walked the JMT, to connect with a great lover of all things; to be moved by the same scenery, to breathe the same air, smell the same scent of the trees and the earth and to hear the same birdsong – to find the heart of John Muir.

Both the Curlew Walk and the John Muir Trail were secular journeys of meaning, answering a desire to get closer to what inspires me. That, for me, is what defines them as pilgrimages: they strum internal strings, resonating and harmonious with a part of life that matters. Whether a curlew-less meadow or a shining granite peak, both hold personal significance. As author Peter Stanford puts it in his book *Pilgrimage, Journeys of Meaning*, 'All such sites are regarded as thin places, set apart from the world, moving to a different drum, and possessed of an innately special atmosphere because of their connection to another, higher dimension. When there, the distinction between visible and invisible can fade, and a door open onto another mindset.'

Pilgrimages can be seen, therefore, as both physical and metaphysical journeys. The same tracks follow the same routes through a planet that is ever in flux, providing refuges for contemplation in the midst of a frantic and confusing world. Our ancestors trod these paths, leaving their fretful and hopeful dreams in the monuments they built across the landscape; the standing stones, ornate cathedrals, secret hermitages and holy caves, all of them speak of a hunger for pardon, for immortality, for otherness, for beauty and a release from fear. They are physical manifestations of enduring human desires. Pilgrimages show that when it comes to the human heart, despite the passing of eras, people have not changed all that much. Author, academic and activist Rebecca Solnit wrote in her 2001 book *Wanderlust: A History of Walking*, 'The walker toiling along a road toward some distant place is one of the most compelling and universal images of what it means to be human, depicting the individual as small and solitary in a large world, reliant on the strength of body and will ... Walking, ideally, is a state in which the mind, the body, and the world are aligned.'

Pitched against heat and cold, wet and dry, hunger, thirst and sometimes pain, some measure of discomfort is built into a long pilgrimage. Indeed, in the past, the spiritual value of the journey was conditional on experiencing discomfort, such as fasting, eating no meat, staying only one night in any location, leaving hair and nails uncut, no warm baths and not sleeping in comfortable beds. It was not enough to simply arrive at a sacred destination, it was necessary to endure the journey to get there. The addition of wolves, bears and snakes added natural jeopardy, as did people with less virtuous intentions. As pilgrimage to Santiago grew in popularity from the ninth century, the rivers of people attracted thieves and swindlers; a guidebook was urgently needed to help navigate the perils. The twelfth-century *Codex Calixtinus*, thought to have been written by the French scholar Aymeric Picaud, is considered the original. Alongside a description of the routes, it includes sermons, a guide to the works of art, a list of miracles performed on pilgrimage and a description of local people. Of the Camino Francés it says:

> *The pilgrim route is a very good thing, but it is narrow. For the road which leads us to life is narrow; on the other hand, the road which leads to death is broad and spacious. The pilgrim route is for those who are good: it is the lack of vices, the thwarting of the body, the increase of virtues, pardon for sins, sorrow for the penitent, the road of the righteous, love of the saints, faith in the resurrection and the reward of the blessed, a separation from hell, the protection of the heavens. It takes us away from luscious foods, it makes gluttonous fatness vanish, it restrains voluptuousness, constrains the appetites of the flesh which attack the fortress of the soul, cleanses the spirit, leads us to contemplation, humbles the haughty, raises up the lowly, loves poverty. It hates the reproach of those fuelled by greed. It loves, on the other hand, the person who gives to the poor. It rewards those who live simply and do good works; And, on the other hand, it does not pluck those who are stingy and wicked from the claws of sin.*

Those are worthy claims, setting the tone for medieval pilgrimage, but few modern pilgrims would identify as sorrowful penitents or devout lovers of saints, and there is certainly luscious food on offer. The intensely religious aspect of the Camino is less important today than a more diffuse spiritual or secular quest. Some walk for the historical interest of the route, for fitness or for cultural reasons. The travel industry has created a niche market, offering spiritual succour without danger or discomfort.

It is possible to stay in boutique hotels and have your bags transported ahead each day. Others opt for a cheaper experience by carrying rucksacks and staying in crowded dormitories with shared bathrooms and the possibility of bedbugs. Increasingly, cycling is a preferred way of covering the miles. But whatever the motivation, standard of luxury or mode of transport, some elements of the *Codex* list above still apply and are carried in many hearts a thousand years later.

Self-imposed endeavour is only part of the picture. Pilgrimages are also touch-points for unexpected kindness and friendship with strangers. They fulfil wishes, provide time for self-reflection, and test endurance. Some of those who walk the network of Caminos believe they have been given a divine mission, like slaying demons or converting the lost, and they actively seek out travellers they feel need their help, whether it is wanted or not. And there are those drifting souls who cannot drag themselves away from a way-marked life. Known as 'Camino Orphans', they spend much of their lives on the narrow road in a never-ending quest that is destined never to be completed. I am to meet all of these characters at various points, spread thinly over the 500 miles, but on that October morning in 2020, the road across the Pyrenees is quiet and I am alone.

Steep climbs dominate the first day; towering, misty mountains rise all around, cloaked in woodland and dotted with farms. Their disposition is kindlier and softer than the jagged Alps, but they still have an edge and can claim lives. With the weather closing in, the lower of the two routes is recommended. Clouds cling to the ridges and creep ever lower down the slopes as rain begins to spatter the road. The route meanders through the province of Navarre, past hill farms with butter-coloured cows, which lumber towards the fences in greeting. They seem to like company and having their noses stroked as their hot, tangy breath mists the air. Curiosity and innocence are held in their dark eyes, and their gaze is as gentle as a soft touch. These cows are destined to be beef; petting them feels like a betrayal. Farm animals have always been part of the Camino, right from its beginnings. These quiet bystanders appear in miracles and travellers' tales as mute witnesses to the endless churn of history, at times they are key players in religious tales of redemption. They carried burdens, were bought and sold, and they were sometimes poisoned or stolen by the increasing number of ne'er do wells preying on the river of holy souls, as the *Codex Calixtinus* warns:

> *This region ... has some truly vicious toll collectors. They come at pilgrims with weapons and demand an exorbitant fee. If you refuse to pay, they'll beat you up and take the money, even intrusively frisking you to get it. These people are forest savages. Their hard faces and strange language strike terror into the heart ... On that mountain, before Spain was Christian, the pagan Navarrese and Basques would not only rob pilgrims to Santiago but mount them like donkeys and then murder them.*

It sounds terrifying, but there is nothing but peace as the empty road winds upwards and onwards. A red kite floats on a bed of air overhead, its gaze fixed on the farmland far below, the first of many over the following weeks. Birds, butterflies, flowers, trees and even rocks give succour when walking alone, but there are modern dangers for creatures with ancient instincts. A metre-long western whip snake lies across the road, the middle of its green and yellow body flattened by the tyre of a car or motorbike. I stoop to look at it for a while, to wonder at its form and lament its death. Its front half is untouched, and its small head rests on the ground as though it is watching and waiting, but its centre is ruptured and its hemi-penes (sex organ) protrudes through the skin. Its spine has been wrenched and twisted by the force of the tyre so that the bottom section of its body is flipped over and faces upwards. I posted a photo on Twitter™ with a sad emoji face, and someone quips that a dead snake might be a biblical omen, perhaps about the pilgrimage slaying evil. The snake isn't evil; to me, it is beautiful.

Human wickedness is a terrible burden to place on snakes; all our ill-intent crammed into a tight, flexible reptile. Instead of being in awe of a creature that can combine whiplash speed with utter stillness, Christian tradition sees only malevolence dripping venom from an evil heart, fit only for casting out, crushing or turning into stone.

> *When Whitby's nuns exalting told,*
> *Of thousand snakes, each one*
> *Was changed into a coil of stone,*
> *When Holy Hilda pray'd:*
> *Themselves, without their holy ground,*
> *Their stony folds had often found.*

Sir Walter Scott's poem about the Saxon abbess St Hilda celebrates the legend of her turning an 'infestation' of snakes in Whitby in Yorkshire into stone and then casting them over a cliff into the sea. You can see the petrified snakes today as the fossils of the extinct *Hildoceras bifrons*, one of the most common species of ammonite found on the shore. The 43 miles of the pilgrimage known as St Hilda's Way, from Hinderwell to Whitby Abbey, is a chance to contemplate the meaning and legacy of saintliness overcoming evil snakes whilst watching white gulls soar over the ocean, dipping their wings in honour of Hilda's miracle. A carving of St Hilda in St Mary's graveyard in Whitby shows her standing on coiled snakes, their bodies crushed beneath her bare feet, as the Camino whip snake was flattened by a vehicle. In another example of the demonisation of these reptiles, St Patrick famously drove snakes from Ireland to make it a country fit for Christianity. The fact that snakes were never in Ireland is not the point. Ever since the devil in the form of a serpent tempted Eve to take fruit from the forbidden tree in the Garden of Eden, we have needed a scapegoat to blame for our wretchedness, and that has fallen to the finely honed tube of muscle and venom that is the snake.

Myths are written to be transmissible through the generations and are often rich in references to the natural world, drawing from its wellspring of form, colour and behaviour. Their aim is to make sense of right and wrong, truth and falsehood, selfishness and love and what separates humanity from the divine. Some creatures come out of this process well, others are demonised and bear the brunt of our darker side. A creature that moves without limbs, kills with poison and can disappear into dark places was bound to come out badly.

According to the doctrine of signatures, plants bearing a physical resemblance to parts of the human body can be used by herbalists to treat ailments of those body parts; by extension, the twisting stems and flowers of viper's bugloss were thought to be an antidote to snake bites, which were apparently a common problem for pilgrims. Its flower's style resembles a forked tongue and its stem is spotted like some snake skins. The seed looks like the head of a viper, and the flower resembles a viper's open mouth, ready to strike. Viper's bugloss is a very snaky plant. Along with black mullein and goldenrod, viper's bugloss is dotted along Camino roadsides, field margins and motorways, brightening a grey, autumnal day. It is a pity we have lost the language of wildflowers, the ability to associate them with daily life. For much of history, they were the fragrant aides-memoires that brought extraordinary tales to life; stories that were rich in metaphor and meaning. For those who knew how to read them, they helped reflect on how the past intersects with the present and informs the future, floral food for the soul.

The tall spikes of both black mullein and goldenrod reminded those who knew their Old Testament of the magical wooden staff carried by the prophet, Aaron – both plants were also known as Aaron's Rod. As a high priest, he used it to proclaim messages, to perform miracles and to exert his spiritual authority. This wondrous piece of wood astonished onlookers by spontaneously bursting into flower or, more alarmingly, a snake. I wondered if the wooden staff that I had seen in the café could channel magical powers, like Gandalf's staff in *The Hobbit* and *The Lord of the Rings*. Perhaps it too could glow with supernatural energy and send fire streaming from its tip. In some religious faiths, wooden staffs are so important they are considered quasi beings.

Pilgrims walking the Shikoku Henro, a 750-mile, 88-temple walk in Japan, traditionally take with them a square-sectioned wooden staff, or *Kongō-zue*. This potent companion represents the body of Kobo Daishi, an eighth-century monk who founded the Shingon school of Buddhism in Japan and is greatly venerated. At the end of each day's walking the staff's 'feet' are washed and it rests inside with the pilgrim during the night. Those who give pilgrims food and water for their journey do so in double amounts to provide for Kobo Daishi, too. Inscribed on the staff are the words, 'We Two – Pilgrims Together.'

As a weapon, a companion, an aide, a symbol, a channel of the divine – wooden staffs were, and for many still are, integral to pilgrimage. In long-lost Christian practices they also took an important role in blessings, especially benedictions given to those setting out. Author and theologian Nick Mayhew-Smith has gathered a range of prayers and rituals for all times of the year and for all manner of occasions in his book, *Landscape Liturgies*. Before leaving on a pilgrimage, it was customary to use the walking staff to pray for safe travels. By using it to draw on the ground, the pilgrim would recite:

I encircle myself by this rod and deliver myself into God's allegiance, against the sore sigh, against the sore blow, against the grim horror, against the great terror, which is loathsome to everyone, and against all the loathsome mischief which into the land may come: a triumphant charm I chant, a triumphant rod I bear, word-victory and work-victory: let this avail me, let no nightmare mar me, nor my belly trouble me, nor fear come on me ever for my life.

It is a heartfelt incantation, which draws together the many fears that stalked the hearts of those setting out when the world away from home was fraught with dangers. I feel some of the fear myself in the autumn of 2020 when the world is dominated by a killer virus and after a long and disturbing lockdown.

Medieval pilgrimage was never taken lightly. It was a journey of danger to the ends of the earth, and it must have felt like an expedition both to touch the glory of the heavens and to explore the pilgrim's own, very human heart. Early travellers faced fears both physical and psychological, and a staff was a comforting and a necessary companion.

Having two walking poles to spread the burden helps me cover the ascending, undulating miles along farm tracks and minor roads to a supermarket and shopping complex on the border of France and Spain, where the trail meets the main highway. The blue and yellow Camino sign points through the car park and past rows of closed shops. Fashionable, expensive clothes adorn bored-looking mannequins gathering dust behind glass windows and bolted doors; they look useless, even pathetic. The supermarket is open but caters more to hunters than to pilgrims. Everything the modern game-shooter could need is on display, alongside a comprehensive range of cow bells. I wander around for a while looking at the camo-clothing, knives and ammunition, equipment needed to provide partridge, hare, pigeon, quail, deer and boar for the pot. Game is a mainstay of Navarrese cuisine and the autumn shooting season is underway; distant gunfire had been a soundtrack all morning.

The last few hours of the day are a slog up a steep, muddy, slippery forest trail that never seems to end. Monastero di Roncisvalle (Roncesvalles Monastery), with its welcoming bed and offer of food, still feels a long way off. Rain is falling steadily and water rushes down the path of least resistance, which happens to be the walking trail – a brown stream swirls around my boots. The humid air subdues the birds, and the weak light filtered by leaves gives it a green tinge; I feel like I'm walking through thin, tepid cabbage soup. On and on it goes until, eventually, light appears at the end of the tunnel and the track once more meets the main highway for a short distance before veering back into the forest. At that point, the junction is marked by a stone drinking fountain, a chance for a drink and rest at the end of the climb, and there, leaning against the trunk of a tree, is the long staff. So, we do meet again. It is still waiting patiently, whilst a diminutive giant fills his water bottle.

There is nothing big or scary about this wiry and welcoming figure, who turns out to be a farmer from Catalan called Joseph; his stature barely exceeds my 1.62m. I guess he must be in his seventies, but it is hard to tell. His face is chiselled and brown from a lifetime outdoors, and his honed physique tells of years of physical labour. He looks comfortable and at home amongst the trees, rocks, rain and the mountains. After an exchange of greetings and a drink, we set off together for the last handful of miles. His staff held upright extends far above his head. It looks ridiculously outsized, but Joseph handles it with ease, the small sack is slung over his other shoulder. His simplicity and lightness make me feel over-prepared and self-conscious. Between my appalling Spanish and his faltering English, we develop a warm relationship full of knowledge gaps and companionship. He tells me he rarely finds the time to break away from his farm for more than a week, but he has completed the whole Camino many times in small sections, and each journey was special. Every so often he stops to eat leaves or flowers he spots on the trail, and he has a pocket full of chestnuts, which he plans to eat for supper. He hands me one, a small, natural token, which will become a treasured keepsake at home. Woodlands and verges are his food store, providing sweet and bitter herbs, fruits and berries, nuts, seeds and mushrooms; the Camino itself is an ever-ready supermarket for those in the know. In past times, when people had a more fluent conversation with the natural world, their surroundings were familiar friends and free ingredients for dishes could be found everywhere. Wild foraging must have been a mainstay for earlier pilgrims, and they probably looked like Joseph. Walking ahead of me is an ancient soul; had he been dressed in different clothes he could have stepped out of the past. I admire his light stride, his acute attention to the life around him, and his gentle smile at the end of a tiring day.

Eventually, the path raises us onto the highest point for this section of the trail, the Puerto de Ibañeta (door of Ibañeta), at 1,100m. Mountain-weary pilgrims would once have been welcomed at a medieval hospital and refuge here, but that has long gone, relocated to the lower and less exposed hamlet of Roncesvalles. A large cross and the modern chapel of San Salvador now sit on the summit, and Joseph and I rest under its eaves before the final descent. I lean against my rucksack and eat a bag of sweets while Joseph chews on flowers. Rain-laden clouds allow only eerie glimpses of the surrounding peaks, and mist hangs around the boulders and crags. It feels cold and desolate, and the first pangs of loneliness descend.

The history of the pass is fused with this sombre scene. Fierce battles are said to have been fought here, most famously in 778, when legend tells us that Roland, the military general and nephew of the emperor Charlemagne (King Charles), was making his way back to France when he and his battalion were slaughtered by

the Basques in an act of revenge for their attack on the
Basque city of Pamplona. The encounter is immortalised
in an epic poem, 'The Song of Roland'. As his soldiers
are butchered, Roland sounds his horn, made from an
elephant's tusk, to call for help from Charlemagne, but it
is too late.

> *Count Roland lifts the horn up to his mouth,*
> *Then sets his lips and blows it with great force.*
> *The hills are high; the horn's voice loud and long;*
> *They hear it echoing full thirty leagues.*
> *King Charles and his companions hear it sound.*
> *The king declares, 'Our men are in a battle.'*
>   *…*
> *Brave French, I see you die on my account,*
> *And I unable to protect your lives!*

Legend has it that if you sleep out in the meadows at
the foot of this pass on the anniversary of the battle, way
down near Roncesvalles, you can hear the screams of
the dying and the clashing of swords in the dead of
night. Other battles have been waged here over time,
ambushes where the rocks must have been wet with
blood as well as rain. It is my first encounter with the
violent history of the Camino, where blood is soaked
into the very meaning of the trail, intermingled with
hope and love.

Mountains are more than geographical borders between
different communities and cultures. All manner of stories
are folded into their crevices. Memories of the past and
strainings of the soul hang like clouds over mountains.
They are powerful gathering places for ambush and death,
for sure, but also for hopes and dreams of crossing them in

safety to travel to faraway places. Their holiness is elevated too. Across the world mountains are the homes of gods and ancestors; sacred, otherworldly temples where the divine comes to meet us.

Layer upon layer of sacredness crown mountain tops, adding to their grandeur. Christianity melds with pre-Christian beliefs on the summit of a conical mountain tipped in white quartz – Croagh Patrick in County Mayo in the west of Ireland. Before Ireland was Christianised by St Patrick, the mountain was used for rituals and ceremonies, a place where hierophanies took place, and the remains of a pre-Christian hill fort can be found at its base. It is said that St Patrick climbed this pagan landmark to battle for Ireland's soul and spent 40 days and nights praying on its barren, sharp rocks. Today, Christian pilgrims walk to the summit in bare feet to meditate on his faith and courage. Whether St Patrick ever set foot on this hill or not is less important than the meaning given to reaching a high place where the sacred can dwell.

Joseph's staff is waiting in its familiar pose, leaning against the stone altar in front of the chapel. Why, I ask, does he need such a long walking stick? His face breaks into a smile so bright it disperses the haunting clouds, and I have a feeling I am about to be given a demonstration. As we set off downhill to Roncesvalles he stops at a particularly steep section, turns around 180 degrees and places the staff firmly into the uphill path in front of him. Leaning into it, he begins to walk backwards. After a few steps his shoulder finds a comfortable notch, and he settles his weight more securely forwards, leaning up-slope. His body and the staff now form a triangle, with the rocky track as the base. He then begins to trot backwards, all the while leaning into the staff, which drags along the ground, providing stability. Occasional glances behind keep him from tripping as he gains nerve-wracking speed. So, this is one use, accelerating downhill in reverse. It is as astonishing as it is amusing, and a moment of delight. He laughs and waves to me to catch up and give it a go. It is a surprisingly good technique, especially for the knees, but hurtling backwards, unsighted, down a steep slope takes more courage and energy than I can muster this afternoon and I hand it back. That playful moment sums up Joseph: an eccentric, good-natured farmer from Catalonia, a soul infused with a deep desire to be a pilgrim and lightened with a twinkling sense of fun.

As the grey clouds are washed with the colours of sunset, the imposing Augustinian monastery, refuge and church of Roncesvalles comes into view and dominates a clearing in the forest. It is imposing, somewhat austere, even prison-like, offering security as well as promising comfort. Set around a central cloister, the high, thick walls and church tower are a reminder of the smallness of the human form. If you were to draw it from this high vantage point, your pencil would immediately sketch out solid rectangular blocks around a sunken green space. The monastery was built on the orders of the bishop of Pamplona in 1132 to provide for the increasing stream of pilgrims. Over the centuries, many thousands of exhausted, hungry, frostbitten, injured and diseased travellers were taken in as they came down off the mountain. If sick, they were allowed to stay for three days, and if they died, they were given a Christian burial. Atop the monastery roof sits the unusual and rather beautiful Roncesvalles Cross. Unlike a standard cross with straight horizontal and vertical arms, the top of the vertical is bent over into the shape of a shepherd's crook, and a symbol of a gourd or a scallop shell dangles from the tip. It combines a walking staff with a cross, marking it as an emblem both of faith and of the practicalities of pilgrimage.

It is a relief to check in, offload my pack and change out of my boots. As my aching muscles find some relief, the great bell of the monastery begins its evening tolling, as it has done for centuries, a sound-guide to draw pilgrims from the dangers of mountains to the safety of its stone walls. The rhythmic clanking draws to the surface deep feelings of being part of something immense that stretches back in time and goes on into the future, that is both visceral and multi-dimensional, but I can't find the right words to express what that means. I know I am just one of many who have felt that tolling resonate deep in the chest. The bells, the wind in the trees outside my window, the footsteps on stone corridors and the soft murmur of voices are sounds that echo out of the past and bring pause to the activity of the day. The journey has begun.

CHAPTER TWO

Moors and Myths

The unmistakable voice of Donald Trump blasts from the TV in full-on raging, cajoling, insulting campaign mode; some look on with horror, some with hope. The American elections are just weeks away, holding out the possibility of a new era in which Trumpism might give way to the quieter politics of Joe Biden, but no one knows for sure which way it will go. Trump jostles for headlines alongside Covid and the January deadline for Brexit, for the United Kingdom to leave the European Union; just occasionally, climate change makes it to the top of the running order because of storms, flooding or fire. Even by the autumn, it is already clear that 2020 is set to be one of the three warmest years on record. This potent mix of hate and fear surrounding world events means that October sees a planet in a crisis of confidence, and anxious about its future. Global storms are rocking the slow boat of the Camino – pandemic, climate instability, political manoeuverings and firebrand populism – they form the disturbing maelstrom surrounding the stone walls of Roncesvalles, and their presence is keenly felt, even in the quietude of a centuries-old monastery. I haven't yet been away long enough to feel one step removed, and anxiety levels are just as they had been a few days earlier in Bristol.

Watching the news update on the rapid spread of Covid across the world, doubts surface about walking the Camino now, of all times. The United Kingdom had one long lockdown earlier in the year, which took out the spring and early summer, and the virus shows no sign of going away, quite the opposite. Many people are self-isolating and lonely, families are being kept apart, older people, and those with medical conditions, are trapped inside to face this horror alone. It feels self-indulgent to take to the road. On the other hand, pilgrims have always walked through uncertainty, in times of plague and war, through epochs of upheaval when it must have felt like the wrath of God could never be appeased. Perhaps, in the past, that was part of the reason they left the safety of the known; to walk to distant, holy places in an attempt to persuade an omnipotent deity to be merciful to a sinful world. It is strangely self-important to believe that God can be influenced by the efforts of one feeble mortal, but that is the audacity of Christianity. Appeasing the Almighty isn't my motivation for finding myself in Roncesvalles on a rainy October evening, even in 2020 in the midst of a pandemic. For me, walking the Camino de Santiago means at last being allowed to realise a dream. For so long the idea had been there but it was always crowded out by other priorities; with every passing year, though, it had grown stronger. And so, as lockdown lifted, a long stint of work was completed, and before the next tranche begins – and because I feared the opportunity may not arise again anytime soon – this felt like the right moment. A tiny window of opportunity had been offered, and so I packed a rucksack and left.

Tradition has it that the answer to the question, 'Why walk a pilgrimage?' is the multi-layered, catch-all answer, 'Prendre du recul,' which means to gain distance and perspective by moving away from the norm. Caught up in the complexity of daily life, it is easy for the detail to dominate at the expense of the big picture. By stepping back to get an overview, life can become more manageable and finds a context. I wanted to walk alone and to let my thoughts synchronise with the rhythm of one step at a time. It feels natural to face a crisis by walking. In an article in the *New Yorker* in 2014, Ferris Jabr brings together the extensive science behind walking, physical and mental health, mental processes and creativity. Research shows that exercise lights up the brain, stimulates neural connections, enhances a positive mood and keeps us mentally alert. He concludes:

> *Walking at our own pace creates an unadulterated feedback loop between the rhythm of our bodies and our mental state that we cannot experience as easily when jogging at the gym, steering a car, biking, or any other kind of locomotion. When we stroll, the pace of our feet naturally vacillates with our moods and the cadence of our inner speech; at the same time, we can actively change the pace of our thoughts by deliberately walking more briskly or by slowing down … Because we don't have to devote much conscious effort to the act of walking, our attention is free to wander – to overlay the world before us with a parade of images from the mind's theatre. This is precisely the kind of mental state that studies have linked to innovative ideas and strokes of insight.*

I like the idea of being visited by ideas and insight, but why a pilgrimage specifically as opposed to one of the many long-distance walking trails that snake across Europe? That is a harder question to answer. Deep inside I want to test the mettle of a faith I had been born into but struggle to fully accept. Too much about Catholicism as an institution rankles. Its male hierarchy, sexist dogma, exclusivity and its seemingly callous rejection of people who are non-binary or divorced; none of these are what love looks like to me. And yet, its heart, the essence of the Christian message, is beautiful. It is a faith based on compassion that embraces the poor, the lost, the sick and the lonely, that understands what failure looks like out on the streets and inside each heart. I have seen it in action numerous times at the forefront of need, working at the coalface of despair, and I want it to step up now, to be present and wise at a time when it feels like humanity is falling apart. This isn't a religious pilgrimage as such, but it is one that will question and search religion for much-needed answers.

Most of the Camino is through countryside, away from main centres of population, providing a chance to be outside in a natural setting and alone, something the American poet and essayist Wendell Berry believes is necessary to become 'coherent within oneself'. After weeks of a national lockdown, inner coherence was not something I or, I suspect, many others, were experiencing. The underlying anxiety about illness, death, our broken relationship with nature and even the future of humanity itself, is a load many of us bear. It is reinforced by the now-familiar closed shops, face masks, hand sanitisers and the new phrase on everyone's lips, 'social distancing'. Even the air we breathe has taken on a dangerous, threatening aspect. The angst of the last few months feels raw. One of my notebook entries for the day reads, 'I feel restless but not sure why, I feel nervous, but don't know why.' I'm hoping the agitation will subside with distance travelled, but even in the ancient, solid monastery, modern technology lets the outside in, and the television news feels like an assault on the soul.

The brash, shouty voices stand in stark contrast to the quiet chapel of St Augustine in the monastery cloister. This is my first, full-on encounter with the Christian Camino, the heart of why it exists. Up until now, my experience has been one of constant organisation for travel and accommodation, finding the right way-marked path, looking for open cafés, petting cows and admiring pilgrim trinkets in the windows of closed shops. But this is different. The medieval monastery is a rock-solid reminder of the Camino's religious core. Its long history, the continued presence of Augustinian monks, the atmospheric cloisters with their hushed presence, all these offer a stepping back in time, a glimpse of its soul. As I walk around the outside walkways and through heavy, wooden doors, I marvel at its size and dedication to purpose, a place set aside, and I feel a shift in gear. Some unidentified weight is being lifted and a pale shaft of light is entering the gloom. And then, I find myself in a tomb.

A combination of bone-chilling, cold air, weak light filtering through stained glass, and the smell of stone-dust, create an atmosphere that is fitting for the chapel of an ancient warrior. King Sancho VII el Fuerte (the Strong) of Navarre (this region of Spain) died in 1234, and his effigy lies on a plinth in the centre of the room. Dressed in armour and wearing a crown, his legs are crossed in the pose of a knight, with one hand resting on his sheathed sword, the other on his heart. For a man who led a life of power and slaughter, he is sleeping peacefully. The sculpture seems a little too large, but in real life Sancho was over seven feet tall, a fact confirmed by recent investigations of his skeleton. His sheer physical presence must have added to his fearsome reputation. It is said he rode into battle on specially bred mules because ordinary horses couldn't take his size. This is the swashbuckling soldier-king who switched allegiances and created pacts to suit his ambition. He slaughtered invading Muslims and fellow Spaniards alike, as well as raiding nearby provinces.

Visible reminders of his life are found all around the room. Casting a motley pattern onto the cream stone, a huge stained-glass window shows King Sancho (or is it St James?) in action. He is centre stage on a white horse, a vast army behind him as he charges into a mass of cowering men with dark skins, presumably representing Moors (Muslims from north-west Africa who were of mixed Berber and Arab descent). Arrows are flying; one man lies in the foreground with one in his chest, his face shows the terror of death in battle. It is a dramatic and bloody scene. Sancho is the handsome warrior king, the fearless leader of men. Beneath a window, on a velvet red cushion, lie the rusted links of a large chain. They are, purportedly, a section of the very shackles that bound slaves together to form a line of defence around the tent of the leader of the Muslim invaders in southern Spain, Muhammad al-Nasir. In 1212, at the decisive and infamous battle of Las Navas de Tolosa, it is said that Sancho cut through this ring of men, took control of the caliphate's tent, and stole an emerald as the single most ostentatious piece of plunder. It was a turning point and prefigured the expulsion of Muslim forces, whose power was already in decline. From then on, King Sancho adopted the motif of chains and an emerald as the Navarrese coat of arms.

The long, complex relationship between the Islamic world and Spain began in the eighth century and ended in the fourteenth. The occupation was at times described as 'golden', with the invaders bringing religious tolerance, learning and the expansion of culture. At other times, it was brutal and oppressive, especially in the thirteenth and fourteenth centuries, when the Muslim rulers were losing their grip on power. Spain's relationship with Islam is woven into the Camino, its traces left in statues and stories all along the trail from the mountains to the plains. At times the violence of this history re-emerges from under the surface and is painfully at odds with this walk of peace. It is distinctly awkward that the holy destination of the Camino itself, the Catedral de Santiago, is dedicated to, and allegedly houses the bones of, a Christian saint also known as Santiago Matamoros, or St James the Moor Slayer. This name is based on the myth that, 800 years after his death in AD 44, St James miraculously appeared at the battle of Clavijo and helped the Christian King Ramiro I of Asturias to victory over the Islamic forces. The valiant saint materialised amongst the failing, outnumbered army carrying a white banner and riding a white horse. Upon seeing him it is said that the Christian soldiers cried out '¡Dios ayuda a Santiago!' which means 'God help St James!' While the story goes that 5,000 Moors were killed and the Christians won the day, historians in fact doubt that the battle of Clavijo ever took place. The first documented reference to it is from 300 years after its supposed occurrence. But, as is so often the case, the truth of the story is not the point. Myth eclipses history.

Throughout Spain, images portraying St James in full battle mode and urging the Christian army to victory are as common as they are unedifying. They take the form of paintings, altarpieces and statues, and invariably show the saint seated on his white steed, sword raised, whilst cowering or beheaded Moors are scattered all around. Gruesome and out of place in a church, they are disturbing, bizarre pieces of art, but as St James is the patron saint of Spain and embedded in the national identity, the iconography is there to stay.

Other strange tales swirl around Moors and their time in Spain. In the small town of Carrión de los Condes (Carrion of the Counts), about halfway along the Camino, a legend persists that the Christian town was made to pay an annual tribute to their Muslim overlords in the form of 100 virgins, to include 50 noblewomen and 50 from the lower classes. The townspeople prayed to be freed from this burden, and their pleas were answered by a herd of bulls who drove the Moors away, leaving the town's virgins in peace (or, at least, in peace from the Moors). As with the battle of Clavijo, the virgin story has little to anchor it in fact, but its truth is not necessary for its power as propaganda. Many layers wrap around this folk tale of Spanish Catholicism, and certainly Islamophobia is one of them. As Catholic theologian Professor Tina Beattie wrote in a personal communication:

> *The idea of sexually predatory Muslim men sating themselves on the pure flesh of innocent Catholic virgins probably helped to keep alive all sorts of resentments and prejudices. But the story is also suffused with yearnings for liberation and redemption. The saints, symbols and sacraments of the Catholic faith become the narrative resources through which cultures tell their popular histories, weaving together memory, legend, fact and fantasy around the central figures of Mary, Jesus and the saints.*

The holiness and the purity of virginity – almost exclusively female virginity – is found throughout Christianity, placing a heavy and damaging burden on women. The image of bulls driving away the dark forces that are attempting to defile womanly innocence plays to the stereotype of strong, righteous men defending their vulnerable womenfolk. It presents such a potent image that it has persisted through the years, and it appears in every Camino guidebook.

The fraught Muslim-Christian relationship took another turn in the twentieth century when the Galician dictator General Franco revived the mythology of St James in the Spanish Civil War between 1936 and

1939. He seized upon the iconography of a powerful Spanish hero empowered by a Christian god to expel invaders to return the land to purity. St James was *the* traditional Catholic warrior. The Camino Francés had fallen out of use from the sixteenth century but experienced a revival as adoration of St James was reawakened by Franco. A steady stream of pilgrims once more began to flow towards Santiago, gathering momentum as the twentieth century rolled on.

Today, these two great religions are periodically locked in an ideological conflict, which at times manifests in actual violence. In 2004, four bombs were detonated on packed commuter trains in Madrid. Nearly 200 people died and 2,000 were injured. The attacks left Spain reeling, and the whole of Europe in shock. Even today, no one knows for sure who was responsible, but many people linked the attacks to the Islamist terrorist group, al-Qaeda. Indeed, they did claim that they had carried out the bombings, although this has not been verified. In the turmoil of the aftermath, it was suggested that the statue of the warring St James be removed from the cathedral in Santiago to help calm the situation and to seek harmony and understanding with the Muslim community in Spain. The proposal was met with fierce resistance. Church officials declared that historic masterpieces should not be removed just because of an unfortunate event. Counter arguments state that the Moor-slaying depictions of St James are re-enactments of a mythical event and it is not unreasonable to suggest that their continued presence could be seen as inflammatory. The statues remain.

Leaving King Sancho to the peace of his tomb, I walk around the corridors of the cloister, which forms four sides of a square. The very word cloister has its roots in the Latin word '*claudere*', meaning to seclude and close-off from outside dangers, and that is what it feels like, a safe place for prayer. The roof above the walkway gives protection from the weather, but the colonnades are open and look onto a garden, or garth, divided into four sections and with a central fountain. The rain has stopped and a vast, starry sky hangs above, its awesomeness and immensity framed by the cloister walls. Confinement and infinity merge in the geometry of a cloister, providing a visual representation of the very nature of monasticism. My footsteps echo off the cold stone; it is a solitary place in failing light. Ancient cloisters hold in their very fabric a sense of noble decay, an enduring, quiet austerity. They were, and still are, places of slow, silent, contemplative walking, and study known as *lectio divina*, or divine reading. Introduced into the monastic way of life in the sixth century by St Benedict, *lectio divina* is not reading in the usual sense of the word, rather, it takes a phrase, even a single word, and examines it slowly and in detail. Thomas Cranmer, archbishop of Canterbury during the reign of Henry VIII, invited participation in *lectio divina* in the following terms, 'Let us ruminate, and, as it were, chew the cud, that we may have the sweet juice, spiritual effect, marrow, honey, kernel, taste, comfort and consolation of them.'

I feel that I am following in the footsteps of generations of hooded, cowled men who chewed the cud of scripture and lived out their lives within this cloister of silence. This was not meant to be a place of chatter and friendship, but one of quiet, inner understanding. Sweet-scented flowers and herbs would once have filled the quadrants, enlivening the senses as well as the soul, layering another dimension to inner prayer. White blooms for purity, red for blood, purple for passion, cruciform leaves for the symbol of the cross – nature playing out the drama of the Christian story in carefully tended flower beds. Stone, water, plants, sky and intercession anchored monastic hearts to both the earth and to heaven. But whatever flowers they chose are long gone; just a vestige of that time remains in the outline of borders and worn flagstones, which are now covered in a tangle of grasses and weeds. The present monks don't carry on the garden tradition, but it doesn't take much imagination to fill this empty space with all manner of scents and floral richness.

Pellitory-of-the-wall hangs in delicate tresses from cracks in the stone, as it has done for millennia on walls and buildings all over Europe. According to the medieval doctrine of signatures, where a plant's shape or habits defined its medicinal properties, Pellitory-of-the-wall became a cure for kidney stones, clinging as it does to rock, being 'a most efficacious remedy in stone, gravel, dropsy and suppression of urine'. The herbalist and apothecary, Nicholas Culpeper, recommended it be mixed with honey and spread over bald heads to encourage hair growth. In hard times, people ate the raw leaves, hence one of its names is wall-lettuce.

In some areas of the Mediterranean, people looked to its flowers for a divine sign. Pellitory was gathered in May, on the Feast of the Ascension, and hung on bedroom walls until the feast day of the Nativity of the Blessed Virgin on 8th September, giving it the folk name of the herb of the Madonna. The plant usually retained enough sap to allow the tiny flowers to open for these few months, an event that was held to be of great significance. The opening of a cut flower was taken as a blessing that the lives of those who had placed the flowers there were viewed favourably by God. If, on the other hand, the flowers remained closed, it was a sign of God's displeasure.

Pellitory was an intermediary between the divine and the human; as it slowly died on a bedroom wall, it dispensed either hope or heartache.

So much meaning was wrung from this common, unpretentious flower. Looking at the soft green of its small leaves against cold, grey stone, I can see why food for thought could be drawn from a plain herb in a barren setting, drawing its sustenance and its healing powers from sterile rock. The gentle bubbling of water from the chalice-shaped fountain in the middle of the square is also a source of contemplation. More than decoration, fountains carry great significance in many faiths. In Christianity, an endless bubbling up of water into a still pool represents the mystery of the Holy Trinity, the Father, the Son and the Holy Ghost; the three manifestations of the divine in one being. Sylvia Landsberg, the renowned garden designer who died in 2021, wrote of the symbolism of water in monastic gardens: 'The three states of water, namely the bubbling, sparkling source or spout, the shallow, moving sheet, and the still, silent pool.'

Echoing off the walls and filling the cloister in an understated but persistent way, the spout of water sings a timeless song and provides another direct link to the past. It is a sound the monks would have heard, and still hear, every day in monasteries around the world. The fountain is open to the sky, to the golden rays of sunlight, to the silver-wash of the moon, it never ceases to gurgle, splash and babble. Sitting as it does in the middle of the garden, it is like the sun around which we mere mortals process like stars. This ancient symbol of the source of life is centre stage in a cloister; it cannot fail to draw connections between the eye, the ear and the heart.

After my time with King Sancho and pondering on his complicated relationship with Islam, the monastic cloister garden takes on a deeper aspect. Both of these great faiths have much in common, reflected through the design of their prayerful green spaces. Both Christian cloisters and Islamic gardens adopt a similar, quadrant template, with a defining boundary wall and a central water feature. In Islam, it is called a *charbagh*, a garden divided into four by channels of flowing water which meet in a central pool. The origins of this design go back 5,000 years to ancient Mesopotamia, now Iran and Iraq, where the idea of paradise emerged from the aridity and heat of the desert as a cool, green, protected space. Indeed, the word 'paradise' is a Persian word for walled garden; it is the place where the faithful will spend eternity.

Both monastic cloisters and Islamic gardens are controlled spaces where a human soul can reach out to an infinite God. In both, nature is harnessed as a living diorama to aid prayer, where only natural sounds intrude upon the silence. But when it comes to walking as part of meditation, as it is in a Christian cloister, why is the design square and not circular? It is more natural to walk in a circle; there are no 90-degree turns to break up a regular step and disturb the pattern of thought. Curved meanderings represent life's twists and turns and the nature of nature itself. Rounded, circular and curled designs date back to some of our earliest artistic expressions; they mimic our thoughts as they spiral outwards, curving round and through and over each other, interlocking and intertwining, to return to the starting point, to the centre of irreducible mystery. Straight lines and geometric forms are not common features of the natural world; the squareness of cloisters seems incongruous. Nick Mayhew-Smith studies the earliest expression of Christianity in Great Britain, and it turns out, early prayer places were, in fact, organic and rounded.

> *The pattern for early monastic churches in Britain and Ireland was not square, it was very different, they were almost always a circular enclosure, called a* llan *in Welsh. This is the root word for both 'land' and 'lawn' in modern English too, so it's a deep-rooted concept and is a prototype for a sanctuary, enclave, wildlife reserve, churchyard and other forms of specially demarcated space. The* llan *usually pre-existed the church itself, and there are many which have a grove of ancient yew trees encircling the space, a landscape configuration that the Christian church rather sympathetically and carefully preserved, and continued to honour …*
>
> *So Roman patterns of building came to dominate monastic architecture of course, with their square enclosures much like a domestic or palatial courtyard, but there is a circular type of cloister that exists to this day … and one I cherish very much!*

The Anglo-Saxons had a related word to *llan*, '*friþgeard*', which roughly translates to 'peace-yard' and is also rich in meaning. '*Frith*' means a state of harmony and calm coexistence, a time without war; it is the peace felt when surrounded by one's own tribe or family, a sense of security within the familiarity of close relationships. But it goes further. Inherent in the word are echoes of the responsibilities of kinship and duty to the wider community, which can extend beyond the human to the natural world. As early Christianity spread throughout Great Britain, it absorbed and remoulded the wisdom within these more ancient beliefs. Paganism, though, had multiple threatening gods which created fear in the growing Christian hierarchy, concerned that worshipping nature would detract from the one true God. The reaction was to cut ties with the natural world. Attention became focussed on the purely human, and references to life came to be understood only in the context of human life. It was a profound, damaging change in direction. In today's age of ecosystem collapse, we would do well to rediscover these ancient, wise concepts and bring them back into our consciousness, notions such as *llan* and *frith*. Their layered meanings deepen our understanding of our interconnectedness, and our responsibility to the living world, and to each other.

It is time to leave the square cloister surrounded by dark mountains and forests, but a last walk around reveals photographs posted onto a wall which show the perils of mountain weather. In 2013, the snowfall was so deep it filled the cloister garden to the height of the roof and blocked the arches of the colonnades, shutting out the light. Snow tumbled through the open spaces onto the covered walkway, but it was not without precedent. In 1600, the original cloister was crushed under the weight of snow and had to be rebuilt. Roncesvalles is situated in a wild, often forbidding place. Bishop Sancho of Pamplona wrote that, 'Many thousands of travellers had died there, some suffocated by the swirling snows, many eaten alive by attacking wolves.' On this October night the winter seems very close, creeping forwards with each passing day. I wonder what the coming weeks will hold and if I am well enough prepared, both mentally and physically. At least for tonight I have a hot meal and warm bed. How brutal it must have been for medieval pilgrims coming down from the mountains as darkness fell, when winter storms were a death sentence. The tolling of the monastery bell over the valley must have sounded like the instrument of an angel. Even today, people die of hypothermia on the high passes, misjudging the path, the daylength and the cold.

King Sancho was a great supporter of pilgrimage, and it was he who ordered the thirteenth-century church of Santa María de Orreaga/Roncesvalles (Orreaga is the Basque word for the area) to be built to service the many pilgrims now arriving at the monastery. A thirteenth-century inscription reads, 'All pilgrims, sick and well … Catholics, Jews, pagans, heretics and vagabonds welcome,' showing that, even back then, a pilgrim was hard to define. When the monks were numerous, they cut the hair and beards of travellers, washed their feet and served them food. Today, with just a few monks living in the monastery, they offer prayers and blessings every evening in the Pilgrim's Mass. The walk from the cloister to the church is a chance to breathe the cold night air and to marvel at the starry sky. A procession of headlights announces the arrival of locals, chatting and greeting each other in the car park. Once through the heavy door, the bustle subsides, to be replaced by a silent, slow, serious atmosphere and soft candlelight. The distinct smell of wax, incense, stone and wood is replicated in churches around the world and always turns talk to a whisper and a settling of reverence. Even amongst the tumbled-down walls and broken rafters of church ruins, vestiges of the old atmosphere remain as people respectfully step over what remains of devotion scattered amongst weeds.

My first impressions of Santa María de Orreaga are both oppressive and welcoming; gold, grandeur and majesty dominate. This is a celebration of the opulence of God, rather than the simple contemplation fostered by the cloister. The sheer profusion of ornate, gilded decoration, the glow of many candles and the wealth of stained glass overwhelm the senses, making it hard to know where to look or to rest the eye. This is a church that was built to impress, to be a marked contrast to the simplicity of ordinary life; a reminder to penitents of the glory of God beyond their reach. The painter Christopher Nevinson remarked that beauty walks an exact tightrope between prettiness and ugliness, a comment that seems relevant to some of the decoration. Statues of saints stare into the far distance, they are ecstatic and transfixed by holiness. The virgin and child sit atop the ciborium, the canopy supported by columns that stands over the altar. A golden mother and child flanked by golden angels glow in the darkness, they are way above us sinners in every sense. By contrast, a simple figurine of St James dressed as a pilgrim stands by a side wall, partly hidden in shadows. He is demure and dressed in a white robe and blue cloak, his hat bears the signature scallop shell, and a gourd of water hangs from his wooden staff. He looks calm and thoughtful. This is St James as a prayerful pilgrim, a simple man of peace and nothing like the sword-wielding Moor-slayer atop a white horse. St James has two faces, ferocious and meek. I can't help but think it odd that he is a pilgrim walking to his own grave.

The tolling of the bell, the chanting of monks, the reverberations from the scriptural readings, the coughing and shuffling of the congregation is comforting. I know this routine well, the format, gestures and words of the Catholic mass are the same anywhere in the world. It isn't necessary to understand the language to mark the place and keep in step inside your own head; the difference in these times of Covid is in the congregation. Everyone is wearing a mask, hiding the lower halves of their faces. From the eyes alone it is difficult to get a full picture of what someone is feeling, especially at a distance. Close-to, the size of the pupils, the extent of the white, the direction of gaze and the movement of eyebrows are all accurate signals about someone's state of mind, but they are not the whole picture. The mouth and facial muscles play a role, too. Looking around I realise just how much I miss seeing people smile, that facial replacement for a friendly hug. Smiling triggers a feedback loop in our brains, both in the person smiling and the person seeing the smile. It suppresses our own facial muscle control, making it almost impossible not to mirror each other, and smiling spreads through a crowd. All kinds of feel-good happens as a result of a smile. Perhaps the widespread use of masks is contributing to our fear; anxiety increasing as the world becomes less smiley. I find myself wishing masks were see-through, it might help ease the burden of this most troubling of times.

We all sit at a prescribed distance from each other, heads lowered to avoid eye contact, increasing the sense of isolation. A few obvious travellers are scattered around, but it is mainly a local gathering. And then one monk begins to sing. Baritone notes rise from the depths, a transcendent plainchant that is unearthly in its yearning, affecting the mood and emotions of the whole church. The words float over the pews and into the rafters, taking with them the hearts of the congregation. Music is a portal to other states of consciousness, to remote, temporary places of heightened emotion. My meandering thoughts are halted, and the restlessness I have been feeling for days begins to still.

Over the centuries the nightly service has seen millions of souls take stock at the thought of their journey ahead. Christian or not, it is an opportunity to mark an endeavour towards something with a personal meaning, be that religious, spiritual, secular or any shade in between. Most who go to these masses are not Catholic, or even believers. As Peter Stanford puts it in his book, *Pilgrimage*, the

Camino has morphed from being a quest undertaken by the devout to an adventure for '57 varieties of spirituality'. Many of them acknowledge their own unique journey here at a religious service, without feeling the need to subscribe to a doctrine.

I had been told before setting out that the Camino was less about the physical road and more about the relationships with people, that walking the Camino is immeasurably enriched by the friendship of fellow pilgrims who bring other ways of living, other life experiences and reflections. Looking around the church that night there are very few fellow travellers. This will be a stripped-down, bare-bones of a pilgrimage at a time of global crisis.

After the service I spend some time with the crisp air, bright stars and blackness. As I walk away from the monastery and into the edge of the woods, with the vestige of plainchant still reverberating, the sense of peace is overwhelming. Trees take on another aspect when lit by the moon and stars; gone are the light and shade, the moving shadows and navigable spaces between the trunks. Indefinable shapes set in insubstantial darkness make knowing what is real and what is imagined hard to separate. It is calming to walk amongst sleeping giants, which is not so far-fetched a notion. Trees droop and revive as they respond to day–night cycles in nutrition and activity, much as we do. Research in 2016 showed that trees 'rest' at night, lowering their branches in a state of repose as their internal fluid-carrying highways relax. In birch trees, this lowering of the limbs can be by as much as 10cm. They are not so different to us. There is something immense about a mountainside of sleeping trees.

Arthur Henry Young, an artist who died in 1943, made a study of trees at night, seeing in their shapes the echoes of human life in all its complexity. His drawings in pen and ink are evocative black-and-white silhouettes full of emotion, straddling the whimsical, the playful, the poignant, the joyful and the tragic. They are a visual poetry of strangeness and splendour; half-seen, half-imagined glimpses of tree people who only emerge at night. Some seem weary and laden by cares; others stretch their branches to the sky in ecstasy. Some look elegant and demure; others are quarrelling and shaking their limbs in anger. Some dance to music that is never heard, embracing their neighbours in joy. All these characters and more are in the Roncesvalles woods tonight.

Our relationship with trees is shifting in this modern, damaged world of the twenty-first century. They are transforming from the 'penetrating preachers' of Herman Hesse, from the emitters of wisdom and good sense to utilitarian absorbers of excess carbon dioxide. We plant them in serried rows over moor and mountain, willing them to put right our wrongs, impatient for their ability to absorb the gases which are changing the atmosphere of the planet. They have become our servants – woody machines, providers of services, with a price on their heads, ready to be harvested and replanted at will. All that we have learned of their lives, how they communicate with each other, live in community, help each other out in times of stress, provide homes for other species, live and die together, compete and cooperate, it all means little when there is a human-made crisis to be dealt with, and when we have identified them as possessing the power to heal. We need them very much, but on our own terms.

Back in the nineteenth century, John Muir fought to protect forests from loggers and developers in the Sierra

Nevada in California. He loved trees with a passion. 'When one is alone at night in the depths of these woods, the stillness is at once awful and sublime. Every leaf seems to speak.' Sometimes, in the dead of night, the leaves do more than speak, they scream. Standing amongst the sleeping trees as the wind scurries through the branches above, memories flood back of a small tent pitched in the middle of giant trees, miles and miles away from home.

Diary entry: John Muir Trail, Sierra Nevada Mountains, California, October 2017

It was late afternoon as I set up camp amongst John Muir's sublime beings on the side of a mountain, pitching my tent in the shelter of a grove of giant sequoias. I felt safer near trees, they towered above, standing guard. I cooked beneath their canopy and rested against a fallen log, staring into their outstretched arms and admired their immensity and their rootedness in this wild Sierra range. Sequoias are true arboreal giants.

A breeze picked up as the evening wore on, which seemed to be strengthening. At midnight I was aware of an increasingly loud roar, as though a juggernaut was hurtling towards me; in semi-consciousness I thought I must have camped in the middle of a motorway. Then the storm broke. Powerful waves of wind funnelled up the valley, ripping through the forests and bouncing off the crags in a fury. They battered my tent and screamed through the ring of trees. After the first wave came a second, then another and another, each as powerful as the last. I put on a head torch and crept outside. The intensity of the darkness was disorientating, and it was hard to stand upright against the wind. My tent tugged at its moorings, trying to break free. I carried as many heavy rocks as I could find to weigh it down and took some inside to secure the inner corners. Fearful and shaking, I climbed back into my sleeping bag, curled into a ball and waited.

The storm raged for most of the night, but by dawn just a gentle breeze played with the pines, acting as though it had no idea what the fuss was about. The sun broke through white clouds and the birds sang like sweet angels. I wondered if it had all been a dream, but scattered debris all around told otherwise. I was overcome with gratitude to the giants. My western brain told me it was ridiculous to say thank you for protecting me, but it felt natural and it was all I could think of to do. Trees are impassive and expressionless in the face of human tears, and these warriors simply stared towards the horizon at something of far greater significance. Facing tempests, floods, wildfire and avalanches are all in a day's and night's work for the forests of the Sierra Nevada, to them, I was little more than an ant.

There is no gale to rouse the trees from their slumber on this autumnal night in the Pyrenees, instead a cold calmness envelops the mountainside. The woodlands feel as known and as unknown as anything I have ever experienced, familiar trees in an unfamiliar setting. The same stars that shine over Bristol look stronger set in a deep, black sky, their light is more penetrating when framed against a forest, city lights sap their power. My spirit wants to stay out for hours, to reconnect and re-remember, but my quickly cooling body yearns for rest. The tremulous call of a male tawny owl floats through the trees, secretive and urgent. It is enough to root me in the present, to call me back. Feeling reassured, I turn for the comfort of the monastery and its steadfast walls with a greater sense of peace than when I arrived.

CHAPTER THREE

Witches and Forests

Rain. The kind that runs down your neck and soaks through the hood of your raincoat, flattening your hair and trickling down your face. Rain. The kind that creates puddles so deep that water seeps through lace holes and over the top of boots. Rain. Spirit-drenching rain. Long before dawn it had battered my windowpane and driving sheets of it are illuminated by the outside lights of the monastery. One brave soul – a woman, I think – is already underway. I watch her from my bedroom, trudging along a walkway. A copious plastic mac covers both her and her rucksack, giving a hunched outline. The beam of her head torch picks out the raindrops bouncing off the pavement. Nothing on earth makes me want to follow. I have blisters from day one and a sinking certainty that my new boots are the wrong size. What felt comfortable in a shop in Bristol feels horrible after 15 miles of mountains. And I am tired. Plumbing the depths for fortitude, I heave on my rucksack and leave the warmth of monastic shelter.

On a sliding scale from 1 to 10, with 1 being the gloomy end and 10, elation, walking alone in the dark and rain before dawn, especially with blisters, sits at around 0.5. I know my mood will lift with the clouds and the inching daylight, but a good hour of wet darkness lies ahead. It was made more uncomfortable by what I had read in the guidebook: that this section of the Camino passes through an area where medieval witch hunts and executions took place. The Way draws all things to itself, the holy, the profane, the beautiful and the despicable.

They sit together on this pathway of human endeavour and there is no way round them.

Quickly, the track reaches the Sorginaritzaga Forest (Basque for Oakwood of the Witches) and I veer off the trail and explore a little. Branches arch over the narrow path to create an arboreal tunnel. Impenetrable darkness and hammering rain accompany the faint squeaking of my rucksack that keeps beat with every step. I try turning off my head torch to see if my eyes will adapt, but I feel vulnerable and trip over tree roots. Torchlight only enhances an uneasiness that clings to the trees and thickens the air. A witches' coven purportedly met here in medieval times, and accusers told of women dancing naked, casting spells and having sex with the devil. In truth, women probably did gather in these remote oak forests to collect medicinal plants, and they could well have practised some ancient pagan rituals that still clung on in isolated communities. Oak trees were revered for their longevity and robustness, which endowed them with particular significance in societies where life was unpredictable and often short. They are still considered sacred in pantheistic religions where everything is associated with the spiritual realm. But even vestiges of this belief cost medieval women dear. Nine supposed witches were burned at the stake in this woodland in the sixteenth century. The terror of these feared and despised women is unimaginable, their hideous deaths inflicted in the midst of the very trees they considered to be protective and nurturing. Their crimes could have been nothing more wicked than healing with herbs, being unmarried or suffering from dementia.

Between 1450 and 1750, witch-hunting hysteria swept through Europe; 300 years of wild suspicion, scapegoating and brutality. Many reasons for the emergence of this era of evil have been suggested; a perfect storm of plagues, famine, bad weather, religious upheaval, widespread poverty and weak governance, which handed too much power to local rulers. Whatever the causes, it was women on the margins, or those who seemed to 'know' things, who most often paid the price, blamed for being conduits for the devil. Many tens of thousands of people (estimates vary from between 40,000 to 100,000) were imprisoned, burned alive, hanged or garrotted; three-quarters of them were women.

Fear of devilry gripped both the popular and religious imaginations of that time, and were amplified by a book, *Malleus Maleficarum*, or *The Hammer of Witches*, written in 1486 by Heinrich Kramer, a Catholic Dominican friar. This handbook on how to identify, extract confessions from, put on trial and execute witches turned the perception of witchcraft as something dealing primarily with sorcery (evoking magic through potions and talismans – something the Catholic Church didn't worry too much about) into the altogether more serious criminal status of heresy. The *Malleus* suggests torture to obtain confessions, and burning as the punishment, the same method as for heretics. Although it was recognised that men could also befriend the devil, especially to gain political power, it was women who were far more likely to fall for Satan's wiles. Women, says the *Malleus*, were 'prone to believing and because the demon basically seeks to corrupt the faith, he assails them in particular'. They were also identified as being weaker in religious faith and more inclined to lust than men, too emotional, superstitious, prone to gossip and feebler intellectually and physically. Kramer believed women 'are defective in all the powers of both soul and body'. The very title of the book *Malleus Maleficarum* is feminine. Given a masculine title, it would otherwise have been the *Malleus Maleficorum*.

In 1525, the Spanish set about extirpating the devilry that they were convinced had taken hold in the wild, pagan-infested mountains of the region of Navarre. A special commissioner was despatched to orchestrate a witch hunt, and he brought with him two sisters aged nine and eleven years old, who were said to be able to identify witches just by looking at them. Apparently, it was the eyes that gave witches away, along with the notorious 'devil's mark', which could be skin blemishes, warts, moles, skintags, birthmarks, scabs, even flea bites – all could be places where the devil stamped his seal. Warts were singled out as the nipples where devilish imps suckled for sustenance. As a sign of Satan himself, these marks were thought to be impervious to pain. The test was to strip the suspect in front of a crowd, and to shave off all her body hair, before silver pins were driven into her skin, even into her vagina, probing for painless areas.

No one knows exactly how many were found guilty of witchcraft and executed in what is now known as the Navarre Witch Trials of 1525–1526, but enough to cause concern within the Church. In response, the Catholic hierarchy stepped into the fray in the form of the notorious Spanish Inquisition, a zealous, organised judicial body, sanctioned by the Pope. It was formed in 1478 to unify the Spanish Church and to rid the land of heretics. Brutal and unbridled as they were in the treatment of converted Jews, who were thought to harbour past beliefs, and those suspected of Protestantism, they brought some measure of order and common sense to the witch trials. They took over court cases for witches from local authorities and imposed a regime where those found guilty were re-educated rather than killed. By and large, this worked, and deaths by execution were reduced considerably, but not entirely.

The Basque Trials, as they came to be known, began in 1609 and ended five years later, and represented the last serious attempt to subdue witchcraft in Navarre. Under the jurisdiction of the Spanish Inquisition, 7,000 people were accused, including many men and children. Despite the large number, only six were burned alive and a further five, who had died in prison, were burned in effigy. Alonso de Salazar Frías, a young judge, was (for the time) admirably sceptical about the flow of absurd accusations that were thrown at suspected witches and of their 'confessions' under torture.

The real question is: are we to believe that witchcraft occurred in a given situation simply because of what the witches claim? No: it is clear that the witches are not to be believed, and the judges should not pass sentence on anyone unless the case can be proven with external and objective evidence sufficient to convince everyone who hears it. And who can accept the following: that a person can frequently fly through the air and travel a hundred leagues in an hour; that a woman can get through a space not big enough for a fly; that a person can make himself invisible; that he can be in a river or the open sea and not get wet; or that he can be in bed at the sabbath at the same time; ... and that a witch can turn herself into any shape she fancies, be it housefly or raven? Indeed, these claims go beyond all human reason and may even pass the limits permitted by the Devil.

As a result of the Inquisition's involvement, witch-burning came to an end in Spain long before it was stopped in more northerly, Protestant countries. Even so, it is a dark stain to add to the many colours of the Camino. As pilgrim Heather Conn wrote in her blog on walking the Camino in 2013:

> *This demonization of women and children is an important, not-to-be-forgotten shadow side of today's Camino de Santiago. The churches and cathedrals along the route easily herald the Madonna in statues, paintings, and prayer as the embodiment of divine, sacred woman. But beneath that glowing halo of Christianity lies unimaginable darkness: the horrific deaths of 'lesser' females, branded as witches, whose lives did not conform to official holy doctrine. This signifies, in extreme form, what Simone de Beauvoir called the long-held cultural view of 'women as Other' in her insightful book* The Second Sex.

Who are today's witches and scapegoats, the easy targets upon whose shoulders we place the ills of the world? Who is being 'othered', and called out to face the revenge of a fearful society? From medieval times to the present day, the white-hot spotlight of blame has fallen on different groups at different times. Women are still victimised, as are people of a different race, skin colour, religion or sexuality as defined by the powerful. Horrors are still visited upon minority groups for what are perceived to be dangerous differences. The term 'witch hunt' references those early centuries and has entered common vernacular as a war-cry to indicate a miscarriage of justice, the chasing down of an innocent victim by a baying crowd. It was a phrase often used by Donald Trump about himself when his integrity and honesty were called into question, which was frequently during his time in public office; it appeared in well over 300 of his tweets.

I am glad to rejoin the main trail and leave the rainy wood, soaked in the troubled spirits of the past. A tall white cross now stands at the forest edge, it looms over the path and in the first hint of dawn it has a faint glow. Far from being comforting, it is eerie. This powerful Christian symbol is a modern version of the original, which was erected in the sixteenth century to dispel the evil spirits that people were convinced haunted the woods. To me, on this disturbing, dark morning, it is a concrete reminder of an era of terrible Christian cruelty and intolerance.

It was not always so. In the early days of the faith, pre-Christian ideas were adopted and absorbed into the new world view. Feasts at midwinter became Christmas. The increasing daylight in February, celebrated at the pagan festival of Imbolc, is now Candlemas. The eggs and flowers of Easter are founded in the many ancient festivals dedicated to the burgeoning of new life. The Celtic festival of Samhain, which marks the end of the harvest and the gathering darkness of winter, was seen as a dangerous time when evil spirits made use of the chaos of the change of season to enter the hearts and homes of the unwary. Those dark forces materialised as witches, which still make an appearance at Halloween in ghoulish pumpkin faces, black hats and plastic broomsticks. The feared hags of Satan are now cheap, chintzy supermarket trinkets. The fact that witches are still part of our lives, even in this diminished, frivolous form, shows they answer a deep human desire to recognise the darker side of our psyche.

Some of the once common adaptations of ancient ideas have been lost in time, and with them their power and wisdom. Æcerbot was a protracted Anglo-Saxon ceremony once used to evoke fertility in the fields. Four sods were taken from the earth and a poultice of honey, yeast, oil and milk applied to the roots. Incantations to Mother Earth were chanted, asking for fruitfulness. The Christian version is similar. Lumps of earth were taken into the church and placed by the altar during mass. They were then replanted with a small cross before nightfall, accompanied by prayers for a rich harvest.

All these examples and more show that at one time Christianity had porous, fuzzy borders, with no rigid, hard-line approach to belief. Goodness and insight were extracted from wherever they were found and absorbed into the unfolding drama of redemption. The seasons, soils, wildlife and even the hard rock of the planet were part of our spiritual journey on Earth. The story of why this stopped can be told in any number of ways, and any telling of it would undoubtedly involve a complex mix of increasing institutionalisation of the church, competition between fragmenting denominations, and the increasing separation of faith and science, which encouraged an abandoning of the old ways. Nick Mayhew-Smith examines Æcerbot and other natural rituals in *Landscape Liturgies*:

> *The full Æcerbot ritual might be a stretch for modern Christians today but it certainly had the full backing of the church in earlier times. Professor Karen Jolly, an expert in the matter of early landscape lore, has argued convincingly that it is meaningless to attempt to distinguish pagan from Christian elements in such early recorded rituals. One could easily claim that the Æcerbot shows hallmarks of pagan survivals from folk magic and superstitions, but the Christian elements are highly pronounced and overt:*

Christian theology and even cosmology are an inseparable part of the ritual language and action. Whether or not you could find a priest willing to offer a church and altar to put it into practice again today is however a moot point. It is perhaps the least likely of all the rituals in this book to see a revival, but its age and overwhelming sense of spiritual power in the landscape alone should give pause for thought, if not a full reconstruction.

Progress builds its empires on certainty; it has no place for a febrile heart's desire and its openness to mystery. But in casting it aside so willingly, we have lost the excitement and wonder of a visceral, earthy recognition of the transcendent, where the spirit world and the everyday weave into something much greater. After centuries of integration and assimilation, the Christian church became Romanised and controlled. We placed Christianity in a rigid box and nailed down the lid.

A faint light is colouring the sky by the time I reach the attractive village of Burguete. A softer rain now falls, a gentler touch after the turmoil of the forest, but by the look of the clouds it is only a temporary relief. Ernest Hemingway had stayed here in the 1920s and wrote about it in *The Sun Also Rises*. He lodged in the central hotel when taking a fishing holiday on the Irati River. Hemingway loved this rugged and remote area for its manly pastimes, including hunting, fishing and the notoriously cruel tradition of bullfighting, which he considered the height of masculinity. Normally, Hemingway devotees join the many Camino pilgrims eating, drinking and resting here, but not this morning. Desperate (not too strong a word) for coffee, I walk the main street, but Burguete is closed. It is as soulless as a filmset. Every door is shut, no lights shine in the windows, no café doors display an open sign to beckon the traveller with the smell of breakfast. The orange streetlights illuminate an empty village.

The village church, dedicated to St Nicholas of Bari, has an austere façade, which seems out of keeping for the original figure behind our beloved Santa Claus. Nicholas, a fourth-century bishop from Greece, was renowned for kindliness and secret gift-giving. He is said to have rescued three poverty-stricken girls from a life of prostitution by secretly dropping bags of gold coins into their father's house to pay for their dowry, the reason we give presents at Christmas and hang chocolate gold coins from the branches of Christmas trees. Praying to St Nicholas is said to assure blessings for sailors, merchants, archers, repentant thieves, prostitutes, children, brewers, pawnbrokers, unmarried people and students. Even more strange, then, that a house of God with a special devotion to a man of kindness saw the burning of five supposed witches right on the doorstep. It is another example of the confused, contrary, compartmentalised, dangerous thinking that dogged the church during the witch trials. Even a short time on the Camino finds the trail littered with humanity's jumbled psychic detritus. As I pick up the way-marked trail out of town, the heavens open again.

There is breakfast to be had in the next village of Espinal, in a whacky café with an upside-down clock and the walls covered in large photographs of caving exploits. They show people dangling from ropes in underground caverns, surrounded by stalactites and strange rock formations. Small figures dressed in overalls and wearing hard hats with head torches illuminate large, black underground lakes, their beam glinting off water whose ripples have never reflected sunlight. On a large television screen, a continual loop of Earth as filmed from the

International Space Station is being shown, accompanied
by David Bowie's high-pitched voice singing *Space Oddity*.
It is an odd juxtaposition, images of the bowels of the
earth next to this glowing hemisphere of blue suspended
in the blackness of infinity. It is even odder to stare at
Earth from on high after having spent time considering
the small-mindedness of medieval witchery. White clouds
drift over the surface of the oceans. The life-protecting
layer of the atmosphere, upon which everything on Earth
depends, looks worryingly insubstantial, as though a tear
might suddenly appear and all the gases we breathe rush
out into space. Technology has allowed us to see what
evolution has not prepared our minds to accept, our home
as an insignificant speck of rock, the famous 'mote of dust
suspended in a sunbeam' of Carl Sagan. All the lines and
divisions, the wars, the cruelties, the politics and the hate
are as nothing when beholding Planet Earth from space.
Astronaut Edgar Mitchell saw this for real through a tiny
spacecraft window, a blue dot drifting further and further
away. He said it gave him what he called 'an instant global
consciousness', humanity as a whole, not fragmented into
countries and further fractured by the politics of division.
The injustices and cruelty that we inflict on each other
seemed ridiculous. 'From out there on the Moon,
international politics look so petty. You want to grab a
politician by the scruff of the neck and drag him a quarter
of a million miles out and say, "Look at that, you son of
a bitch."'

A widening pool of water is spreading across the tiled
floor from my dripping coat and rucksack. The owner has
noticed it too and asks if there are many on the trail, he
looks worried when I tell him I had only seen one person
leaving Roncesvalles before me, and no one had caught
me up. He stands behind a line of cooling, pre-cooked

fried eggs stretched out along the polished bar. Covid is
keeping people off the Camino, depriving the shops and
cafés of vital income. The number of pilgrims has fallen
from over 300,000 a year to virtually none, almost
overnight. Places offering accommodation and hospitality
find the solid foundation upon which they depended
rapidly transforming into quicksand. Anxiety is gathering
along the Camino, adding another layer to the human
drama inscribed into this well-worn track.

My news app tells me that Donald Trump is in hospital
with Covid and is being treated with an expensive,
experimental cocktail of drugs. People are out on the
streets, praying for his recovery. One elderly lady is shown
outside her house, hands clasped in supplication to a God
of mercy, fervour on her face, pleading for his safe return
to the White House. I watch a short video of a dramatic
performance by the American TV evangelist Kenneth
Copeland, demanding the Covid virus submit to the
power of God and be cast out. He claims that by exhaling
loudly he will blow it away with the breath of God, and
he demands it submit by crawling on its belly. It is an
uncomfortable display of evangelical zeal, at once comical
and unnerving to watch. Heavy metal guitarist, Andre
Antunes, underscored Copeland's words and unhinged,
manic laughter with death-metal guitar riffs, blending
fire-and-brimstone rhetoric with a genre of music often
associated with godlessness.

The whole world is out of kilter. There are odd
juxtapositions everywhere; weird behaviours are being
normalised as a reaction to the pandemic. It is nothing new,
though, extreme responses, both religious and secular, have
always emerged in times of fear and feeling out of control.
Attempts to regain a sense of power over the world brings
to the fore all manner of desperate remedies. For Covid,

suggestions include drinking camel's urine or making a tea made from lemon and baking soda. Others promote intense sunbathing or wearing anti-static clothing. President Donald Trump thinks injecting bleach might work, or perhaps we could all try shining bright lights into body cavities. The Camino absorbs it all, it has seen it before.

The Black Death (or bubonic plague), which killed over one-third of Europe's population in the fourteenth century, was spread by pilgrims on the Camino de Santiago. As crowds gathered in the villages and towns along the route, infected fleas jumped between animals and people and the death rate soared. As the transmission of the plague was not understood, theories abounded as to why it was so contagious. Supposed causes were as varied as bad odours, the position of the planets, deliberate poisoning by people of different faiths, divine punishment for sins, the curse of witches, even being stared at by someone who was infected. In order to ward off the evil eye, some pilgrims bought metal badges at holy shrines to wear as protection. Some of these had surprising motifs, including an array of anthropomorphic representations of genitals. Vulvas and penises were shown sporting arms, legs or wings, and they were engaged in all kinds of bizarre activities. Vulvas dressed in a pilgrim's garb rode horses, penises paraded a crowned vulva on a processional bier, vulvas walked on stilts, penises wore crowns, vulvas roasted penises on spits, penises sailed boats across the sea, some vulva pilgrims carried a penis staff. There seemed to be no end to the imagination of the medal-makers. No one knows for sure, but it is thought that the wearer believed these images averted the gaze of the evil forces that would otherwise infect them with the Black Death.

I can imagine the jolly travellers from Chaucer's fourteenth-century story of pilgrimage, *The Canterbury Tales*, wearing these bawdy badges as they sang, joked, flirted and played music together on their long journey. Not everyone was a stereotypical ascetic, many were ordinary people who enjoyed local festivals, music and sex. On feast days, the atmosphere in some of the Camino towns and villages must have been riotous. With the rain falling steadily outside, I wish that one of these rowdy troupes would materialise in this empty, cold café, scoff down the congealed fried eggs and set off again, all chatter and cloaks billowing in the wind – I know I'd tag along for a while.

The discomfort from blisters on one foot is getting worse, and so is the rain. The forest tracks are now small rivers and the puddles have grown to the size of mini lakes. A simple metal plaque supported on three rods tells of 64-year-old Shingo Yamashita, a Japanese pilgrim who died at this point on the trail in 2002. It is one of many memorials along the Camino. Some are miniature shrines with flowers, memorabilia and photos of those who have died. A surprising number commemorate people who were in their twenties, their dreams cut far too short. One particularly moving shrine is to Michael Cura, a 16-year-old who died on a school cycling trip. It quotes from the novel, *The Pilgrimage*, by Paulo Coelho, 'The boat is safer anchored at the port; but that's not the aim of boats.' Other casualties were older, their faded photographs show faces weathered from the many times they had walked the trail on an unending spiritual quest. A surprisingly large number of deaths were the result of car accidents, a common tragedy for Camino cyclists in particular. Quite a few had drowned whilst swimming in the sea at Finisterre on the west coast of Spain, celebrating the very end of their journey. Exertion and summer heat got to many, as did dehydration. It doesn't seem possible as rivulets of rainwater trickle down Shingo Yamashita's plaque, and a deepening chill creeps into my bones. Through the centuries many thousands of pilgrims must have died on The Way with no one to mark their lives. Their quiet spirit is all that remains, somehow defining the path more clearly. I pile a few small stones under the memorial, a modest homage to the forgotten travellers, and walk into the woods.

The Pyrenean hillsides are rich and deep, clothed in a mixture of deciduous trees and conifers. Bears, wolves and chamois are thinly scattered here and even the suggestion of their presence adds a frisson of primordial excitement. Once common, fewer than 70 brown bears now roam these 5,000km^2 of mountains and there are concerns over their isolation and inbreeding. A few bears from other locations have been introduced over the last few years to try to increase the gene pool, but their widespread recovery is opposed by cattle and sheep farmers who fear for their livestock. The same applies to wolves. Having dwindled to fragmented populations in the centre and north-west of Spain, today they number between two and three thousand, but there are thought to be fewer than twenty in the Pyrenees. It seems only right and natural that large predators should roam free in the mountains, but people sit uneasily next to creatures that are untameable. Mountainsides without bears, lynx and wolves are certainly safer for livestock, but some of their rocky soul is no more.

In 2017, I walked the John Muir Trail without fear of grizzly bears, which were eradicated from California by 1924 by farmers fearful for their animals. A subspecies of the well-known grizzlies of Alaska, the so-called 'golden grizzly' was revered for the golden tinge to its fur, and for its power, beauty and ferocity. It was officially classified in

1815 as *Ursus horribilis* ('terrifying bear') and often captured and taken to local towns for the popular spectacle of pitting it against bulls. As people increasingly moved livestock into the mountains during the nineteenth century the bears were hunted to extinction; even so, it remains on the Californian state flag as a proud boast. The less dangerous black bears are still common, but most Americans don't worry too much about them, seeing them as more of a nuisance when they raid rubbish bins rather than as a danger to life. For someone from Bristol, though, they are an arresting sight.

Diary entry: John Muir Trail, Sierra Nevada Mountains, California, October 2017

At first light, with the air still freezing, I packed my camp and went to a stream to wash. Only the sound of the running water broke the silence. Then, a loud crack of snapping wood. Just metres away and looking straight at me, was a black bear. We were both very still. When wild eyes meet ours, the moment of connection is electrifying. I had been told that black bears were curious but easily spooked; if you jumped up and down, shouting and waving your arms, they would run away. In the stillness of that quiet, cold morning, that didn't feel like an option. And anyway, fear had frozen my throat, as had astonishment and wonder. Part of me wanted to run, but another wanted to bury my face and hands deep in its thick, dark pelt and feel the warmth seep into my fingers, which were numbed by the coldness of the river. Its paws were immense. I don't know how long we stood there, then slowly, very slowly, its low-slung head swung away, followed by the heavy body, and it swaggered into the bushes. Rooted to the spot, I watched it disappear with a strange mixture of relief and longing. I try to relive that moment when the oppressiveness of work and inner-city life clamps my spirit and weighs me down. The memory of those black eyes, the sound of the stream, the sharp, grey rocks and the cold air hit me like a wave in the sea and it takes my breath away. I am immensely thankful for the opportunities that have come my way.

Memories of the John Muir Trail often return during the Pyrenean stretch of the Camino, gathering around outlines of mountain tops or triggered by the smell of damp trees. The two walks merge and intertwine in my mind, despite their different characters, remoteness and physicality. Perhaps it is because they share the same motivation: a desire to move through a landscape to explore mystery and to get closer to something of great personal importance, but what that is exactly is difficult to describe. Mountains, for me, hold many associations. They house the spirit of my hero, John Muir, but they also hold the dark clouds of grief. Remote mountains claimed a luminous and gentle soul at the age of 24, someone I loved very much, and I have struggled to make peace with rock and ice ever since. That is part of this Camino journey, too.

The origin of the name Pyrenees is not an uplifting tale. According to one tradition in Greek mythology, Princess Pyrene was beautiful and a virgin (there we are again), the daughter of King Bebryx, who ruled over part of southern France. Bebryx offered hospitality to the infamous he-man-come-demigod, Hercules, when he was completing one of his twelve labours, a series of tasks set for him by the oracle at Delphi to atone for his bad behaviour (no less than killing his wife and children). Unable to resist the charms of Pyrene, he raped her before setting off to complete his mission, stealing the cattle of the three-headed giant, Geryon. While he was away, Pyrene gave birth to a serpent and fled into the forest to hide her shame and to escape the wrath of her father. In despair she told the trees her troubles and as she wept her tears formed the many lakes. Her sobs resounded throughout the mountains attracting wild beasts, which tore her limb from limb.

On his way back through the forest, Hercules discovered her chewed remains. As was often the way with this intemperate lump of muscle, he became filled with remorse and cried out to the mountains, the forests and all the wild animals to join him in grieving. So thunderous were the many cries of *Pyrene!* that they echoed from valley to valley, filling the whole range with her name, which became known as the Pyrenees. There are many variations on this story, but all of them cast Pyrene as the victim of abuse and Hercules as the abuser, who remains a heroic figure today.

One less violent origin story tells of mountain shepherds leaving a campfire alight during the night. The flames spread rapidly, setting the whole range on fire. So devastating was the event that the mountains became known as the Pyrenees, related to the Greek word for fire, pyro.

Fantastical legends, raging fires, battles, massacres, witches and gods crowd around these cow-hills between France and Spain. All mountain ranges draw from us outsized imaginings. Their size, permanence and indifference to our own puniness grants them the status of the seats of eternal beings, such as Abellio who was the most famous of the Pyrenean deities. Very little is known about this Celtic sun god, who was associated with Apollo, but even so, I reckon it is worth petitioning him this morning for some relief from the never-ending rain.

The oppressiveness that had enclosed the witchy wood lifts with increasing distance and the strengthening daylight; and Abellio does oblige as the rain gradually peters out. I slither down a steep bank and put my feet into the rushing water of the River Arga. One blister looks worryingly angry. The water flows relentlessly onwards, tugging at the branches that dip into its tumult, as though trying to drag them to the sea. A few pilgrims are now materialising and a group wave from the track above. I feel more heartened, and even the unfulfilled promise of a refreshment van at a road junction is not an unmitigated disaster.

The final stretch of the day is steeply downhill to the village of Zubiri. In the pale, late-afternoon sunshine a more joyful mood emerges from the gloom. Someone has scribbled on one of the characteristic gold and blue way-markers, 'Walk – don't run.' Not that I can run, but I appreciate the multi-layered messaging. One of my greatest regrets when walking the John Muir Trail was fastidiously ticking off the miles and setting goals for the distance to cover each day. I should have had the courage to sink into the permanence and slowness of mountains, not rush to the car park at the end of the trail. John Muir himself would not have approved.

People ought to saunter in the mountains – not hike! Do you know the origin of that word 'saunter'? It's a beautiful word. Away back in the Middle Ages people used to go on pilgrimages to the Holy Land, and when people in the villages through which they passed asked where they were going, they would reply, 'A la sainte terre,' 'To the Holy Land.' And so they became

known as sainte-terre-ers or saunterers. Now these mountains
are our Holy Land, and we ought to saunter through them
reverently, not 'hike' through them.

'Walk – don't run,' is the first of many sayings, poems
and pieces of art I find daubed in spray paint on
underground passes, old walls and boulders right across
the Camino. Another that strikes a chord is, 'The only
two mistakes that one can make on the road to Truth:
Not starting – Not going all the way.' Fun, meaningful,
trite, irreverent or proselytising, Camino street art reaches
out beyond the churches and monasteries to make
statements more relevant for the modern saunterer.

Other people are staying at the Airbnb™ where I check
in, but I don't see them. My dripping coat and waterproof
trousers hang next to theirs in a covered passageway, but
the warmest spot by a radiator is already taken by a pile of
soggy footwear. My dirty, wet boots are banished to the
cold margins.

Wandering the dark, quiet streets looking for
somewhere to buy food, I find myself back at the twelfth-
century bridge that leads into the town. Its two large
arches and thick stone pillars are still strong enough to
withstand a raging River Arga when swelled by winter
rains and snow. The bridge has its own intriguing moniker,
'the bridge of rabies'. According to legend, any animal
that passes under the bridge three times, or that walks
around the central pillar, will be protected from this
terrible disease. Who knows how these stories came to be,
but it is an indication of how much rabies was feared for
centuries, and often the vector was thought to be wolves,
which were universally hated and feared.

Wolves and pilgrimages are an unlikely association,
but I will come across them again when I walk the Way

of St Francis, or the Via di Francesco, through Tuscany and Umbria in the autumn of 2021. This pilgrimage follows the wanderings of St Francis of Assisi between Florence and Rome, and passes through the town of Gubbio, the setting for the poignant tale of St Francis and the Wolf. Whatever the truth behind the details, it is a story for our times, a tale of reconciliation and compromise, and for finding creative solutions in the midst of human-wildlife conflict.

The story recounts that the people of the hillside town of Gubbio in central Italy were terrorized by a large male wolf which attacked the people and their livestock. No matter what they did they could never catch and kill it; it made going into the woods a matter of life or death. Francis was moved by their plight and so went alone to meet the animal face to face. On seeing him, the wolf lay down at his feet as Francis began to speak. He told the wolf that he knew he was starving and in despair, but, as brother to brother, he must ask him to stop harming the townsfolk and their animals. In return, Francis promised that the people would provide food each day and not persecute him. The pact was sealed as the wolf laid its paw onto the palm of the saint's hand. To the astonishment of the locals, Francis and the wolf then walked to the town centre, side by side. Every day the wolf visited the houses to eat the food left outside, and legend tells us that it never maimed or killed again. When the wolf died, it was so revered it was given an honourable burial and the church of St Francis of the Peace in the centre of Gubbio was built on the site of its grave. Many centuries later in 1872, when the church was being restored, the tomb of a large wolf was unearthed, covered by a stone carved with a cross. The people of Gubbio reinterred the remains inside the church. The pact between St Francis and the wolf showed that a relationship with the planet need not be based on dominance, that peace through compromise is possible, but it needs someone to reach beyond hate to help make it happen.

What a story, I have loved it from childhood. I wanted to be there as the wolf listened to the saint in the cool of a glade. I imagined that even the birds kept their voices down and leaned forward on the branches to eavesdrop. Dr Doolittle and St Francis merged as characters with magical powers that allowed them to chat with animals, to hear their side of the story. There was non-human wisdom to be had and I wanted to be part of it. Gubbio went to the top of a list of must-see places.

Diary entry: Gubbio, Via di Francesco – Umbria, Italy, September 2021

The forest where the encounter was said to have taken place has long gone, replaced by a network of roads, shops and suburbia, and it was down one of these pleasant but faceless roads, right next to a major road junction, that the small, medieval church of Santa Maria della Vittoria sits like an island out of time. Sixteenth-century frescoes adorn the walls and the air inside felt cool. I sat back and closed my eyes.

It took a while for my mind to settle, but when it did there was no peace. Unbidden, the enormity of issues facing the earth seemed to pour in through the windows and the door and uncontrollable tears began to flow. Like the snow tumbling through the porticos of the monastery at Roncesvalles, grief filled the interior of the church with a suffocating, crushing weight of despair. Everywhere my mind wandered it saw destruction and brokenness, wildlife extinction, habitat loss, climate catastrophe, cruelty, eradication. Ecological grief can be so painful it physically hurts. The solutions to the woes of this planet are so complex, so deeply rooted in economic systems built on destruction, that finding a way to release them seems an insurmountable task. The sense of hopelessness and my own impotence was paralysing. And then, in the midst of desolation I felt a gentle presence beside me. I don't know if it was the spirit of St Francis or my own fevered mind inventing comfort, but I was accompanied through the storm by some attendant who understood what it was like to stare into the abyss.

When the rage subsided I was drained, but there was more hope in my heart. The pilgrim paths of the world know we need a place to go to rail against the world's injustices, a safe space to ask questions and seek answers, or to simply despair. They are thin lines of catharsis threaded through a world that often appears overwhelmed by damage and hurt. Pilgrim paths are narrow but they open us to the wide, random sea of humanity in all our magnificence and our failings. I left the tiny church in a suburb of Gubbio knowing something had changed.

Day two on the Camino de Santiago enfolds into its healing ambit the endless throngs of the misunderstood, the persecuted and the voiceless, both human and non-human. The day had started with witches and it ends with wolves, the circle closing at Zubiri's bridge of rabies.

The next morning, I am up early, but my fellow travellers have already left. Someone had thought to put my shoes in the warmest spot, and I am very grateful. I will discover that small acts of kindness are sprinkled along the Camino, sugary sweets for the soul; they are encouraging messages, bidding the receiver to carry on towards whatever lies ahead.

CHAPTER FOUR

To the Stars

The planet under our feet is a fiery, dynamic and restless ball of energy. Stardust coalesced into Planet Earth over four billion years ago and formed a sphere of mobile viscous layers. Ever since these dramatic beginnings, the earth has been cooling down and the thermal activity has caused the fractured, fragmented crust to shuffle around the surface. As the separate plates grind, scrape, collide, override and subduct, they create the earthquakes, volcanoes and the mountains we see today; these are the rich landscapes where life thrives. The earth is always building, forever eroding, constantly depositing sediments and turning them into rocks. All this activity creates a myriad of conditions under which a host of precious metals and minerals form, substances we prize today. One such mineral is magnesite (magnesium carbonate).

Magnesite is coveted in the twenty-first century for its precious chemical cargo of magnesium. Essential for a range of industrial, technological, medicinal and agricultural processes, magnesium is consumed by the modern world in vast quantities. Magnesite mines and processing factories are lucrative places. One of these industrial plants sits on the outskirts of Zubiri, an unsightly area of grey sludge, grey slag heaps, and lakes of grey water. This is important business; the factory employs over 200 local people and has an annual turnover of 88 million euros. More than 300,000 tons of useable forms of magnesium are produced annually in the Zubiri plant and 85 per cent is exported to 60 different countries. It feels odd to be looking at it from an ancient pilgrim trackway, but then the Camino Francés is a line of confluence where deep time, human history and modern life all meet. You enter Zubiri by crossing a medieval bridge and leave it by passing a modern, industrial, magnesium-extraction plant.

For sure, many would call it a blight on the landscape, but I photograph it on my mobile phone, a device that also has magnesium components. Magnesium is an element essential for steel production, animal feeds, medicines, water purification, for the extraction of sulphur dioxide from gases, to line furnaces, and in waterproofing around land contaminated with heavy metals. China is the world's main supplier of magnesium but has recently tightened its exports to protect its own reserves, causing Europe's industrial sector to warn of catastrophic consequences if the supply is compromised. Western Europe is increasingly reliant on European ore, and on extraction plants like the one on the outskirts of Zubiri. As the original mine is virtually depleted, another source has been located very close by. However, it falls within the European network of protected areas called Natura 2000, and, unsurprisingly, there is consternation about the possible environmental effects of opening a new mine in an area set aside for nature. The mining company, Magna, is at pains to point out that they will respect the values of the Natura 2000 Network and that by careful management they will increase biodiversity and enhance the landscape. I can only hope they are right.

As with every resource we use, there is a tension between people and the planet. The presence of the magnesium factory on the Camino is just one of a range of environmental issues that are raised across the 500 miles of northern Spain. Modern farming, forestry plantations, plastic pollution, industrialisation, urbanisation, population pressure, biodiversity loss, climate stress … they are inescapably part of the pathway today. Setting out may feel like taking a step back in time to walk a trackway that holds the past in stillness, capturing history in aspic, but that is far from the case.

On the day I leave Zubiri, low cloud hangs like wisps of smoke over the forested hills, pale and spent. Gone is the insistent rain, but it has left its mark in the wet air and puddles. The greyness is brightened by red and gold murals celebrating the Basque culture, one of the oldest ethnic groups in Europe, dating back thousands of years. The colourful paintings show people in traditional costumes playing atabals (flat, double-sided drums) and the alboka (a type of double clarinet); communal dancing, singing and eating are a hallmark of Basque culture. Navarre is a stronghold of the Spanish Basque region, a proud territory that is holding fast to its language and identity in an increasingly homogenised world, but its public face has been marred by episodes of violence carried out by political separatists in a struggle for independence.

Both Basque and non-Basque people have lived in the Navarre region for countless generations. The twelfth-century Camino guidebook, *Codex Calixtinus*, does not have good things to say about the Navarrese or the Basques; and that is putting it mildly.

The Navarrese and the Basques have similar food, clothes and language, although the Basques have a faire complexion. The Navarrese wear black outfits down as far as their knees, like the Scots. They tie untreated leather scrips around their feet, leaving bare everything except their soles. They have dark, elbow-length woollen cloaks, fringed like a traveller's cape, which they call 'sayas'. Their clothing is visibly shabby.

Navarrese eating and drinking habits are disgusting. The entire family — servant, master, maid, mistress — feed with their hands from one pot in which all the food is mixed together, and swill from one cup, like pigs or dogs. And when they speak, their language sounds so raw, it's like hearing a dog bark.

They call God 'Urcia', the Mother of God 'Andrea Maria', bread 'orgui', wine 'ardum', meat 'aragui', fish 'araign', home 'echea', the head of household 'iaona', the mistress 'andrea', church 'elicera', priest 'belaterra' which means 'good earth', corn 'gari', water 'uric', the king 'ereguia', and St James 'Jaona domne Jacue'.

These are an undeveloped people, with different customs and characteristics than other races. They're malicious, dark, hostile-looking types, crooked, perverse, treacherous, corrupt and untrustworthy, obsessed with sex and booze, steeped in violence, wild, savage, condemned and rejected, sour, horrible, and squabbling. They are badness and nastiness personified, utterly lacking in any good qualities. They're as bad as the Getes and the Saracens, and they despise us French. If they could, a Basque or Navarrese would kill a Frenchman for a cent.

In some places, like Vizcaya and Alava, when they get warmed up, the men and women show off their private parts to each other. The Navarrese also have sex with their farm animals. And it's said that they put a lock on the backsides of their mules and horses so that nobody except themselves can have at them.

Moreover, they kiss lasciviously the vaginas of women and of mules.

Everybody with sense slams the Navarrese. However, they're good in war, although not so effective in a siege. They pay their church taxes and present their offerings to the altar; every day a Navarrese goes to church, he makes an offering to God of bread, wine, corn or something else suitable.

Wherever a Navarrese or a Basque goes, he has a hunter's horn around his neck, and carries two or three spears, which they call 'auconas'. When he comes to his home he gives a whistle, like a bird. When they're lying in ambush and want to call companions quietly, they hoot like an owl, or howl like a wolf. Tradition has it that they're descended from the Scots, because they have such similar customs.

The reference to Scots (and some odd Cornish people too) is found in the book's history of the region, where it describes how Navarre came to exist.

It is said that Julius Caesar brought three tribes to conquer the Spaniards who refused to pay him taxes: the Nubians, the Scots and men with tails from Cornwall. He ordered them to kill all the Spanish men, and to keep alive only the women.

   The invaders came across the sea and, with their ships having been destroyed, devastated the country with sword and fire, from the city of Barcelona all the way to Saragossa, and from Bayonne to the mountains at Oca.

   They didn't get further because the Castilians united, defeated them in battle, and drove them back. They fled and settled in the mountains at the coast ... Then they raped the women and had children with them, who afterwards were called Navarrese.

Perhaps frustration and resentment can go some way to explain this diatribe. The author, Aymeric Picaud, was furious at the exploitation of pilgrims by some locals, something he had experienced first-hand. Exorbitant sums were charged to cross rivers, horses were stolen, people beaten up and robbed – it was not a safe or straightforward journey in the early days. I feel a twinge of umbrage myself at a café on the bridge at the entrance to the village of Zuriaín. Despite a jolly statue of a cartoon-like pilgrim by the door, it is not a welcoming place. There is no obvious menu and I am charged €3 for a small cup of lukewarm tea, the same amount for a full breakfast elsewhere. The man who serves me is short and thin and his friend, seated at a table, is round and bald; they make a Laurel and Hardy-esque duo. Mr Short-and-Thin wordlessly shoves my overpriced tea at me, without making eye contact, then joins his plump companion and both resume watching a large TV, which is screening a quiz show from the 1970s. Tight trousers, thick, downturned moustaches and mullets are everywhere. The speakers blare out tinny tunes and canned laughter from a set that is all bright lights and garish plastic. The scene is so incongruous I sketch it in my notebook. A group of happy Germans are waiting patiently to pay, the only other people in the café. After ignoring them for a good while, Mr Short-and-Thin drags himself to the counter and slaps the bill down in front of them. They leave in a quiet, down-hearted mood.

Outside, a sea-grey wash of colour infuses the air, but as the sun grows in strength and confidence, a yellow hue brightens the surrounding hills and sunlight glints off the wet road. There is more warmth and less dampness now, a sense of change. I like this new weather; it is quieter, calmer, less intimidating. Insects can fly in a straight line and sounds travel further. I now hear birdsong, the faint rustle of leaves, and the barking of dogs from somewhere far away. The world is becoming happy, mud-luscious and puddle-wonderful, to borrow from the poet E. E. Cummings.

On the spur of the moment, I detour onto a different Camino, signposted as the Camino de San Sebastian, which traverses the other side of the valley; it is on more elevated ground and meanders through fields and patches of woodland before meeting the Camino Francés just before Pamplona, today's destination. It feels so peaceful and airy; sweet fennel and goldenrods add a splash of yellow to the grey and green scrub. Then suddenly, from nowhere obvious, comes music from what sounds like pipes, as though the Greek god Pan is sitting in the bushes. Dancing notes float on the wind, the music seems to lift from the vegetation itself. Someone is out there, perhaps in a half-hidden hut by some trees, but why they are playing in a field, and who is listening is not obvious. It is so lovely and uplifting, so much from the heart, that the notes draw to the surface childhood memories of Stoke-on-Trent.

One of the personal possessions I treasure the most is a decorative plate that used to hang in my parents' home, and now in mine. The scene is of a wide valley framed by green hills and white crags, which I am sure are based on the White Peak in Staffordshire. A copse of trees and a few wildflowers add interest to the foreground, but mostly the landscape is bare, with one exception – the dark, solitary figure of Pan. He is in the middle distance, sitting on the side of a hill with his pipes at his lips. Goats' legs, horns, a pointed beard and the suggestion of dark hair on his body place him in the mythic realm of the god of shepherds, wilderness and nature. Half-man, half-beast, he is a bizarre, grotesque character who, legend tells us, craved the love of a wood nymph, Syrinx. Repelled by him, she ran away and plunged into a lake and drowned. The grief-stricken reeds called out as they swayed in the wind, moaning and sighing in plaintive harmonies. Pan was so distraught at losing her that he cut some of the hollow reed stems and, tying them together, for evermore honoured her memory by playing 'sweet, piercing sweet' music.

I have always yearned to enter that scene painted on a plate on the wall of our sitting room, above my dad's armchair. I wanted to sit by Pan and listen to his melodies fill a lonely valley; I still do, very much. Through the strains of musical sadness (or is it guilt or remorse?) I would talk to him of nymphs, sheep and shepherds, and the rolling of time through wild lands. I would ask what it is like to be half-goat, a creature associated with stubbornness and belligerence, but also lust and fertility. Would he have the staring, bulging, unreadable eyes of a goat, or the round, familiar, windows-to-the-soul eyes of a man? Would he bleat or talk? That image of Pan is foremost when listening to the musical pipes dancing on the breeze across the Camino de San Sebastian.

Serendipity is built into the Camino. People who have experienced it talk about it as a character that engages with you as you walk. They stress the road is not inanimate but somehow living and responsive. Today it is being playful. Beautiful tunes float on air washed clean by rain, a musical gift after the dark woods with their ghosts of murdered women. It was Jeff Bezos, the founder of the online store Amazon, who said that serendipity is always a part of discovery, even if it is just exploring a website. It is what made him rich. I've taken a gamble on a lesser-known route and am rewarded by a mini concert. And then, as suddenly as it had started, the music stops.

Mystery and memories keep me going on the wooded descent into Pamplona, past more Basque slogans and the increasing signs of people and habitation. Locals are out walking dogs or exercising, keeping a safe distance from me and each other. Everyone wears a mask. The law in Spain demands that everyone outside their home must cover their nose and mouth. I have been warned that the on-the-spot fines are hefty, and rightly so. The rules reflect the intense worry in Spain about the pandemic. In early October 2020, cases of Covid were rising rapidly. On the day I set out there were 29 million cases worldwide; just a few days later it was 36 million. As yet, there is no vaccine. I had a PCR test immediately before leaving the United Kingdom, and I am staying in solo rooms and most of my time is spent alone and outside. The Camino passes through areas of low incidence of the virus, but further south, Spain is experiencing a surge in cases. Each province decides its own strategy, with some imposing stricter regulations than others, but everywhere it is being taken seriously.

Covid sits alongside the other threats of climate change and loss of biodiversity as the unholy trinity of crises causing existential angst across the globe. The longstanding sacred cows of constant economic growth, development towards westernised lifestyles, and ever-increasing consumption seem at best misguided and at worst wanton foolishness. The economic box we had placed around the planet is slowly disintegrating, proving to be nothing like as secure as we had assumed. The vulnerability of humanity is being exposed. Walking a 1,000-year-old pilgrimage route is not an escape from these home truths, they come to meet you face to face.

The last stretch of the day takes me under the imposing city walls surrounding Pamplona and through a gate into narrow streets. The fortifications prove that this is a city that has seen centuries of hostility and invasion. Once inside, I sit for a while outside the locked cathedral, resting my throbbing blisters. I had wanted to see the famous cloisters and the soaring, gothic ceilings, but Covid has shut religious tourism down and I have to be content with a group of drunken men singing and shouting in the square. Pamplona is bustling in a subdued, practical way; locals are doing necessary business rather than taking time and socialising. A mother and daughter scuttle past, hand in hand, the woman in high heels and a miniskirt, the young girl in a duffel coat that covers her white dress. She also wears the tell-tale white shoes, white veil and faux jewels in her hair, the uniform for girls taking First Holy Communion in countries where traditional Catholicism still holds sway. There are no other pilgrims, no groups of friends chatting, no students or elderly neighbours gathering for an early drink outside the cafés and bars of this beautiful medieval city. A few people nod and mutter 'Buen Camino' as their eyes scan my rucksack, before they too hurry away, faces covered. There is only one exception to the constant movement: an elderly man is sitting on a bench playing an accordion to no one in particular. His head is bowed as his fingers move over the keys. I think he is playing to all of us to give us heart.

The cheap hostel is near the city centre. Check-in is online and access by a keypad. The only person inside is cleaning the floors, but they quickly disappear down the stairs and out into the evening streets. Hand sanitisers are on every floor with large, stern posters stating the rules about distancing and face masks. My bedroom is tiny and stuffy. I take a photo of my reflection in a full-length mirror while wearing all my walking gear as a reminder of what it feels like at this point in the journey. The room is the colour of brown algae with barely enough space for both me and my bag. Facing the window is a small bed, which squeaks and bounces as I sit on it, more of a camp bed than a permanent fixture.

As I lie in the quiet and the gathering dark, shadows dance on the ceiling, thrown there by the streetlights. Half of a sandwich and some biscuits do for an evening meal, but it's enough; on long treks (for me), food is more about sustenance than enjoyment. I am beginning to feel a little queasy from the pain in my left foot, but the discomfort is offset by knowing that I am really on my way. The start of the walk is done, the first range of mountains is behind me, and undulating farmland lies ahead; the well-defined path that is the Camino Francés beckons. I am in an extraordinary city at an extraordinary point in history.

Pamplona is built on the banks of the important River Arga and is surrounded by fertile land, with access to both the north coast and to the mountain passes into France. Throughout time it was desired by many men of ambition who saw its strategic potential. Glory, power, wealth, destruction and hardship are woven through the turbulent history of this most fortified city in the north of Spain. Founded by the Roman general Pompey the Great, who defeated Julius Caesar in 75 BC (described in the *Codex Calixtinus*), it was destroyed by Moorish and Frankish invaders, then became the capital of the Navarre Kingdom by Sancho III in the year 1000, and then conquered by Spain in 1512, which turned the Navarre Kingdom into a province. As with many great cities, violence is part of its historical fabric, especially so in Pamplona.

Spain may now be free of war, but violence is still on show. Just down the street is the glowering presence of the legendary bull ring, the Plaza del Toros. This arena of pain, fear, blood and flamboyant masculinity was built in 1922. It was beloved by Ernest Hemingway, and when he took his own life in 1961, tickets to a bullfight were found in his home. It is still visited by the millions of modern tourists who enjoy watching animals being tortured to death. Hemingway admired the ritual slaughter of bulls so much so that he famously declared that only bullfighting, mountaineering and motor racing were sports; the rest were merely games. He was a complex, tortured character, renowned for his moods, jealousy, deep distrust of women, competitiveness, argumentativeness and machismo. In his novel *The Sun Also Rises*, bulls are multifaceted symbols of passion and power, with the interaction between a bull and the matador thought to represent the act of sex as well as the constant outwitting and warfare that defined his relationships with his friends.

Bulls and Pamplona collide spectacularly in the annual festival of Sanfermines, a nine-day celebration to honour the patron saint of the city, St Fermín. On each of the days, a loud explosion triggers the release of six or more young bulls into the city. Large, rowdy crowds gather to watch them race down narrow streets, terrified and confused. Men and boys dash out in front and try to outrun them in a show of bravado. Every year people are injured or killed by trampling or goring. In the evening, the same bulls are slaughtered in the bullring in a stylised, hyped ritual of torture for which there is no escape for the bull, only a lingering, painful death. It is a horrible spectacle and no amount of appealing to tradition can justify it. Only the sheer number of tourists who flock to see the festival every year keep it alive. Covid restrictions are a welcome respite for the bulls, but tourist money is too important to allow it to fall from favour for good.

The night deepens outside my stuffy bedroom. I try to focus on the more pleasant aspects of Pamplona, like the maze of narrow streets with its many specialist shops selling food and wine. At around midnight, a man and woman enter the room next door. By the sound of their voices they are young, perhaps students or backpackers, and they are drunk. They laugh and whisper, trying, but failing, to be quiet. I have a growing sense of unease at the sound of furniture being dragged across the wooden floor, presumably two single beds being pulled together. The dividing wall between my bedroom and theirs is paper thin. I put the pillow over my head, but it is not enough. I wear headphones and turn the volume to maximum, but nothing can block out the sound of exuberant sex on springy beds. Trying not to hear is impossible, it's like trying not to sneeze. I give up, dress quickly, and go out into the night.

For half an hour, I walk the dark, quiet streets. All the cafés and restaurants are empty, their chairs stacked and their doors locked. The pedestrianised streets are paved with large flagstones and framed by tall apartment blocks. They would normally be noisy with drinkers and diners well into the early hours. When the bulls are running, not only are the narrow streets packed, the balconies are too. The sound must be deafening. But tonight it is eerie and dystopian. Ghostly bulls run up and down the flagstones, silent hooves spurred on by ghoulish, baying crowds. You can't get away from bulls in Pamplona; cartoon bulls stare out of shop windows, life-size statues show them charging at running men stumbling ahead of them, photographs of matadors strutting, swirling, stabbing are celebrated everywhere. It is a gruesome, self-mythologising, disturbing array of horror. Tonight, the streets of Pamplona are full of ghosts.

Modern-day bull-running has its roots way back in the third century, to the martyrdom of St Fermín, or perhaps it was his spiritual master, Saturninus – no one is really sure which. Condemned for professing a Christian faith, either Fermín or Saturninus was tied at their ankles to a bull, and the animal was then set running through the city. For some reason, St Fermín captured people's imagination more than Saturninus, and Fermín became the city's favoured saint. Today, his martyrdom is commemorated by nine days of cruelty to bulls.

Christianity, martyrdom and gruesome deaths go together. For 2,000 years all manner of macabre ways of killing people have been inflicted on those who refused to deny their beliefs; in some places they still are. I find the

ancient stories of martyrdom abhorrent. Martyrs have
been skinned, burned, roasted, impaled, chopped, boiled,
hanged and sliced, they have had their teeth pulled out, their
skin pared away, and, in the case of women, their breasts
cut off. The Catholic Church in particular highlights these
tortures to remind the faithful of what true commitment
to faith looks like. The stories also keep those of us who
benefit from religious freedom in a state of humble
gratitude. Passion, pain, agony and ecstasy are part of
Catholicism's nature. The message is clear – there is no
glorious, heavenly gain without excruciating, earthly pain,
and rapturous suffering is etched onto the faces of the
millions of statues of saints that decorate Catholic churches.
I cannot relate to this joyful martyrdom, I have more
empathy with the trembling, terrified whisky priest in
Graham Greene's *The Power and the Glory*, who has to be
dragged to his execution as his legs crumple beneath him.
It is a strange contradiction – to walk the Camino is to
reflect on the meaning of life in places that are
overwhelmingly associated with grizzly deaths.

By the time I get back to my room my joyous neighbours
have fallen silent, no doubt wrapped around each other,
sleeping peacefully. Perhaps I imagined them, or maybe
they too are ghosts, like the bulls running through empty
streets. Maybe they are spirits of past pilgrims who
embraced all of life on their long journey to Santiago. As
I close my eyes I wish them well; ghosts or not, I am glad
they are there.

They are still sleeping when I leave at first light to walk
the same streets I had wandered through at midnight. A
tall plinth with a statue of St Francis and the wolf towers
over a plaza, commemorating the peace this gentle man is
said to have brought to the city. Did St Francis actually

walk to Pamplona from Assisi, and then on to Santiago?
No one knows for sure. Some stories say it took him two
years; others think it unlikely he ever made it this far.
There is no concrete proof, only suggestion, hearsay and
stories passed down through the ages. Even so, a small
walking stick said to have belonged to St Francis resides
in a glass cabinet in Santiago. Myths, legends, facts, fiction,
canny marketing, deep desire – they all play into the
stories that accrete around the Camino.

It is getting harder to ignore the pain in my foot now; I
am limping badly. Each step is difficult, especially on the
hard surfaces of the university campus and through the
suburbs of Pamplona. I can't be deterred, though, I'm on
a mission. The first of three journey markers I have circled
on the map is within touching distance, and I am
determined to see it. Just a few miles away is the Alto de
Pérdon, the Hill of Forgiveness, the high point of a long
ridge, with a sculptural installation showing a train of
pilgrims through the ages. I have seen it in numerous
books and in the film *The Way*. Something about its airy
position on the boundary between contrasting landscapes
and the stories of love and tragedy that swirl around the
summit make it stand out as a highlight. The first
milestone is so close, I'm not about to let blisters stop me.

Concrete streets eventually give way to huge,
unpartitioned, undulating, freshly ploughed fields, creating
a vista of brown and red soils fringed with green grass set
against a deep blue sky. In the distance are tantalising
outlines of hills and mountains. Gone are the forests and
rushing rivers, this is the start of the Rioja region; rich
farmland put to work to produce vegetables and the
famous wines. The stony track cuts through the landscape,
a light brown artery, bordered by alfalfa, fleabane and
chicory; all of them have their own stories to tell. Violet

alfalfa, introduced into Europe in classical times from
South East Asia to feed cattle, has roots that can reach six
metres downward into the soil to tap water. Fleabane is
the colour of the sun and smells like carbolic soap, a
natural insecticide that was hung in houses or stuffed into
mattresses to keep fleas at bay. And my favourite, blue
chicory, with its beautiful, toothed petals and roots that
can be dried and ground to make ersatz coffee; its large,
bitter leaves add a daring taste to salads.

How some associations with the natural world came
about are often lost in time, and dried chicory provides one
example of strange connections. Supposedly, it has the
power to open locked doors, but only if it is harvested on
Midsummer's Eve at midnight, or on Midsummer's Day at
twelve noon, and only if a golden knife is used to harvest it.

Two young German women resting on a bench in the
sunshine say hello as one of them examines her own
painful feet, and we exchange sympathetic smiles. They
are sitting by another memorial cross, this time to a
Belgian man in his sixties, Frans Joseph Koks, who had
died from a heart attack at this point in 2004. A photo of
Frans with his rucksack sits in the intersection of the
horizontal and vertical arms of the cross, and below is a
Star of David. Frans was loved and missed, and his loss
inspired others to walk the path. A beautiful, faded note
wrapped in a clear plastic bag has been carefully placed at
the foot of the cross.

Hi Frans,

At last I have arrived here. It is because of you that I
have started this trip.

You have chosen a beautiful place to start that other
journey, but without saying goodbye to your wife and
children. I will do that for you, when I am back.

Everything is going well with them, Frans. With your
wife An, and with Kris, Martine and Michel.
    See you again on that other Camino, Frans Josef.
    Cees Merksplas and Jos Beuse

Before long I enter the ancient village of Zariquiegui, just
below the climb to the Alto de Pérdon sculpture, a sign
written in capital letters in Basque, Spanish and English
reads, 'WE DO NOT TOLERATE SEXIST
AGGRESSION IN ZARIQUIEGUI.' This village was
ravaged by the Black Death in the fourteenth century,
emptying it of residents and pilgrims alike. It is now
battling both Covid and, it seems, antisocial visitors. What
awful sexist aggression has happened here? A more pressing
question for me right now, however, is how I can carry on
walking with this searing pain in my foot. I sit on the wall
of the medieval church and steel myself. Slowly, carefully I
take off my boots. My left sock is soaked in blood and my
foot is so painful I cry out when re-dressing the blister.
Putting my boot back on makes me feel sick and my foot
feels like it has been in a meat grinder. But the Alto de
Pérdon, the Hill of Forgiveness, is right in front of me.
    On the outskirts of the village is a small, ancient well
and drinking fountain nestled by the side of the road.
Like thousands of other sources of water, holy stories
bubble around it; fantastical, salutary, hopeful and life-
giving legends that endure through the centuries. Their
longevity can be attached to the overarching message that
transcends the details of the stories themselves. This
fountain has its origin in a battle of wills between a holy
man and Satan. We are told that many moons ago an old
pilgrim was dying of thirst as he began the climb to the
top of the Hill of Forgiveness. Suddenly, a figure appeared
by his side and offered to give him water, but only if he

renounced his faith. Seeing through the disguise, the old man refused, saying he would rather die of thirst than sell his soul to the Evil One. The devil disappeared in a flash of indignation. As a reward for his faithfulness, St James now appeared to him in person and revealed a fountain of water, sips of which he gave to the pilgrim in a scallop shell, the symbol of the Camino.

There are so many stories of this ilk, all of them with a moral lesson that encourages us to be vigilant, not to give in to the easy option, to be wise to false promises, and to be assured that commitment to our own values will be rewarded. It is a message I need to hear, and so I gather my courage, ignore my foot, and begin the half-hour ascent.

The 700m climb to the top is one agonising step after another, but the views are wonderful. Bathed in sunshine is the sprawl of the city of the bulls and the wider countryside of Navarre. Northwards, the high mountains show a hint of snow on their peaks; beyond them, hidden from view, is the sea. The wind is strong but enlivening, or it would be if I felt better. The last section is particularly steep and painful, and I can feel my spirit straining to keep going. Peter Stanford's book, *Pilgrimage, Journeys of Meaning*, describes these long trails as having a spiritual and emotional geography as well as a physical one, with both metaphorical and physical highs and lows. This stretch is my nadir. I arrive at the famed sculpture feeling as though I can't go on. Despite the elation at standing next to my first way-marked goal, I want to give in and go home. My joy and inner strength have been drained by pain. Seeing me trying to take a selfie, a woman who had just parked nearby offers to take my photo. The sculpture was installed in 1996 and depicts a caravan of life-sized pilgrims through the ages, from early medieval to modern, and they all stride purposefully westwards towards

Santiago. I am so happy to be next to it, but when I look at that photograph now, all I can see is my face etched with distress. The woman wanders around a little, then drives away, and I am left alone. I take some time to study each figure in the line.

There are 12 in all, the first seems to be searching for the right path and symbolises the beginnings of pilgrimage. The following group of three illustrate the growth in numbers as the walk to Santiago became more popular in medieval times. Next come tradespeople and merchants hawking their wares to the ever-growing flow of people. Then, a solitary figure, a woman, indicates the decline as pilgrimage fell out of favour. There is a gap before two modern figures illustrate a revival in pilgrimage from the middle of the twentieth century.

It is this break that frames the backbone of the ridge, which stretches away into the distance. Atop is a line of 40 huge, white, whirling windmills, which have dominated the walk up from the valley. Like a white Mohican, they line the ridge crest, cutting across the path of the Camino. Built in Navarre in 1994 by Energia Hidroelectrica de Navarre, which also commissioned the sculpture, they are unnatural sentinels to a modern era of climate crisis. It is no surprise to find them installed here, as a constant, strong wind blows across the Alto de Pérdon from the south. They are massive, each windmill is the height of the Statue of Liberty, noisy and imposing. The blades slice the wind, transforming it into electricity that supplies Pamplona. Until they were built, Navarre imported all of its energy, now this is just one of a number of green projects across the province.

Like the magnesium factory, the windfarm intrudes into the quiet contemplation of the Camino, a powerful reminder of the climate emergency. The droning, whirring and straining of the machinery cannot be ignored; the windmills demand that we consider our lives of high energy consumption. They are sympathetic companions to the art installation at their feet, which appeals to the simple, spiritual journey of individuals through the ages. The link between outdoor art and modern technology is thought-provoking. Some complain the windmills are an eyesore on a World Heritage pathway, but for me they are 40 signs of hope in exactly the right place. There is nowhere better than a long pilgrimage to consider what we are doing to the planet and how we can arrest overconsumption, overuse of resources and overpopulation. It also seems apt that the turbines dominate a hill dedicated to forgiving the sins of humanity. Built straight over an ancient trackway they provide a clear, hopeful demonstration of our potential to renew our relationship with the earth.

Traditionally, pilgrims who climbed the Alto de Pérdon would have reached the Basilica of Our Lady of Pérdon, a hospital and refuge, but they are long gone. Monks and priests would have dispensed absolution for sins, the misdemeanours of the true penitent blown away by a cleansing, spiritual wind. Freed from this burden, travellers were assured that even if their bodies failed before they reached Santiago and they died en route, their spiritual health had been restored. That is some comfort as I contemplate the steep descent on an increasingly useless foot.

The metal figures are marching westwards over the top of the Hill of Forgiveness, heading down to the exquisitely named Valley of the Stars, which is laid out in the afternoon sunshine far below. Whoever thought of these names had an ear for landscape poetry, and it is echoed in the evocative title of the sculpture, *Donde se cruza el camino del viento con el de las estrellas*, which translates as, 'Where the path of the wind crosses that of the stars.' How lovely is that image; the same wind that has blown the capes and coats of pilgrims throughout the ages also buffets the eternal shining spheres in the sky.

Then, another sign catches my attention, but this one is so shocking all thoughts of poetry are quashed. The plaque stands alone and is set away from the main track, just before the path downhill. It faces a garden of standing stones designed to mimic the ancient stone circles found across western Europe. The heading on the information board is in both Spanish and Basque and translates as, 'Always in our memory.' The English text reads:

> *This memorial symbolizes the recognition and reparation for the 92 people assassinated in 1936 and 1937 by the Francoist repressive regime, after the coup d'état against the legitimate [partly scrubbed out] government, in Sierra de Pérdon.*
>
> *This is a tribute to the victims and their families who were killed for fighting for their ideals of social justice and democracy. In Navarre there wasn't a front during the war and these people were killed without a trial, deprived of their homes by force and buried in mass graves in this land. All of them forgotten and silenced for 81 years by the institutions.*
>
> *The memorial includes a stone in the middle which symbolizes all those who disappeared and other [sic] 19 smaller stones arranged in an open spiral which represent the villages, towns and cities where part of the population was murdered.*

The names of the men and boys are listed, the youngest was 17, the oldest 57. A photograph taken during the excavation of one of the graves shows jumbled human bones and, especially moving, the sole of a single shoe, the underside facing upwards. It is deeply distressing. The years of civil upheaval in Spain in the 1930s, where

Republicans fought against Nationalists, resulted in bloodshed and atrocities across the country. Whatever the complex politics, the human face of war is concentrated in that photograph of just one mass grave among many found scattered across Spain. In front of the plaque stands the circular monument representing the dead and the villages where they once lived, silent and immoveable against the force of the wind. The suffering goes on in the memory of those who are still alive, who carry the scars of those terrible days not so long ago. The walls of Pamplona, the magnificent castles and fortified buildings right across the Camino might give the impression that war is safely in the past, but this photograph is a reminder that it is always close at hand, just beneath the surface of respectability. The human cost is terrible to confront.

The steep, stony and skiddy descent kicks up rocks and pebbles, and every one that bounces off my boots causes waves of pain. At the bottom, a large stone bench offers a resting place, it faces a shrine dedicated to the Virgin of Irunbidea. A woman is already seated there, deep in prayer, her head bent. A white statue on a plinth shows Mary standing on a serpent that seems to be screaming in its death throes. It was given to the locals by a pilgrim who stopped here feeling too tired to continue. He recalls meeting a young girl called Maria who was so gentle and encouraging, it is said that she gave him the courage to carry on to Santiago. I will come across a very similar tale further along the trail, but for now, this story gives me sufficient courage to reach the centre of the village of Uterga. And then I stop. Any further attempts at being brave evaporate. Every ounce of determination is gone. I collapse onto a wooden bench under the symbol of the Camino, a yellow scallop shell set in a blue background, and know I can go no further. There are only six kilometres left to the end of the day's walking, but I cannot do it.

I know I look the image of abject defeat because a builder working on a roof nearby shouts over to see if I need help. I nod and point to my foot and tell him I want to get a taxi to Puente la Reina (Bridge of the Queen). He takes out his phone and I am flooded with gratitude. A finger post tells me I have only walked 60km from Roncesvalles and there are over 700km to go to Santiago. It seems impossible I will make it now. While I wait for the taxi, two playful cream and lavender kittens appear, they both have extraordinarily blue eyes. One of them bounces over my rucksack and stares at me inquisitively. They jump and play, tumble and frolic, and they prove I can still smile.

As the taxi speeds along the main road, I watch the Camino wind its way through vineyards and trees. I am so angry with myself. I feel stupid for letting a blister get so bad; I am furious it is ending like this, and so soon. I am particularly sore as I had planned to detour off this stretch and visit Eunate, a mysterious, isolated church set in the middle of fields. No one knows exactly when it was built, who built it or why, and now I have missed my chance to explore it for myself, let alone reach the cathedral in Santiago. When I check in to the hotel, the receptionist examines my face while I fill out forms and looks concerned; she carries my bag to my room.

We have always depended on the kindness of strangers, and by the end of the day the hotel has made an appointment with the local doctor for early the next morning. At least I can get treatment before heading home, because by the look of my foot, that is the only option. The Camino has dished out so many experiences in the few short days I have been on the road, and now it is done with me. I put my head in my hands and cry.

CHAPTER FIVE

The Kindness of Strangers

The doctor stares at me with cold eyes and a look verging on contempt. In good English, she asks why I let the infection get so bad? Antibiotics, daily dressings and rest were the only options, she says, it is up to me if I want to continue the walk. I know what she is thinking, and I agree – I'm experienced enough to know better and I have no excuses. But at least I am holed up in the delightful town of Puente la Reina and in the friendly Hotel Jakue.

When I was planning this trip, seasoned Camino walkers told me to forget about having fixed ideas, timetables or goals. 'The Camino might have other plans,' they would say, with a knowing look. Any long journey that relies on muscle power is slow and is dictated by health and fortune; clocks and timetables have very little to do with it. This isn't the way we do things in the West today, where travel relies on safety and reliability combined with comfort and speed. Using the body alone to travel a long distance is counter-cultural; twenty-first-century legs are considered obsolete when there is motorised transport on offer. This is satisfying for those who want to swim against the tide for a while, but the whole venture comes to a halt when the feet at the end of those legs fail. And so, with no other option, I submit to the whims of fate, lie on a bed and wallow in self-pity. But I have been here before.

Diary entry: John Muir Trail, Sierra Nevada Mountains, California, October 2017

After carrying a heavy rucksack for nearly three weeks, I noticed a strange feeling and some weakness in my right shoulder and arm, and my hand seemed to be detached from my brain. Soon afterwards, the pain started – a searing, shooting pain that was so intense that it made me cry out and I was forced to let my arm hang motionless by my side. Backpacking alone at 3,000m above sea level was tough enough for me, but with only one functioning arm, I was on the edge. I had two options. The first was to dig deep and carry on for a further three days to the top of Mount Whitney and at an altitude of 4,400m; the official end of the trail, followed by a 7-mile walk out. The second was to admit defeat, hike for a day to a remote road and then try to hitch a lift to the nearest town. Later that evening, when the pain of trying to set up camp and to cook reduced me to tears, I decided to call it a day. There was an older woman who had camped not far away, and I asked her if she could spare some painkillers, as mine had run out. As she found some pills the size of horse-tablets, we chatted about plans. She was walking a short trail of five days, I told her I was planning to bring my 230-mile JMT to an end the following morning. She fixed me with a stare: 'No, lady, you are not giving up! You haven't come all the way from the Yosemite to quit now. You will never forgive yourself. *Finish* it!' And so, I did finish, and I am grateful to her. Sometimes it needs someone else's determination to drag to the surface the last bit of grit. It took 18 months for a weak arm and a paralysed finger to recover from what turned out to be brachial neuritis, but recover they did, and I have the memories of Mount

Whitney that will stay with me forever. It was a lesson in not taking the easy option, in giving in to the inner whisper of weakness.

Soon after that encounter, late in the afternoon, I walked to a high point near the campsite as a blood-red sun hung over the western Sierra mountains. The sky turned an ever-deeper shade of blue as towering, flame-tinged clouds glowed atop the razor edges of the peaks. It was breathtaking. The intensity lasted just minutes, but the sight was seared into my soul. John Muir saw this, I am sure of it, and described it in his own inimitable way:

> *What can poor mortals say about clouds? While a description of their huge glowing domes and ridges, shadowy gulfs and canyons, and feather-edged ravines is being tried, they vanish, leaving no visible ruins. Nevertheless, these fleeting sky mountains are as substantial and significant as the more lasting upheavals of granite beneath them. Both alike are built up and die, and in God's calendar difference of duration is nothing. We can only dream about them in wondering, worshiping admiration, happier than we dare tell even to friends who see farthest in sympathy, glad to know that not a crystal or vapor particle of them, hard or soft, is lost; that they sink and vanish only to rise again and again in higher and higher beauty.*

I draw on that JMT experience to consider where I am on the Camino, whether I let pain stop me in my tracks, or give it time and then carry on; but I know time is not on my side. Covid is building all around, as is winter, and who knows how long this pilgrimage will be possible. Giving up is unthinkable. I know there is more wonder ahead, that a slowly unfolding and deepening complexity will be revealed, and each difficult decision is part of it. And for sure, there are many simple moments of kindness to keep the spirit going.

The Camino enables kindness, gives it a home and allows it to be. Small deeds, gestures, offers of help, a smile, a gentle word – they make walking the 500 miles seem more like floating downstream. Being on the receiving end of a kind act is transformational. The warmth of kindness revives goodness buried within, melting the hard, protective shell that seems to be a consequence of modern life. Kindness is infectious, it inspires kindness in others, multiplying its effects, which ripple outwards to who knows where. Kindness is subversive, rebellious and anti-establishment. It is unlegislated for, anti-capitalist, often unacknowledged, but it runs through society. We are bound together by it, buoyed by it and carried through by simple acts of everyday kindness.

Kindness does not require a spotlight or expect a return, and it does not need a reason to exist. It is an open-hearted expression of humanity that is freely given to all, and because it is driven by the integrity of the giver, it requires no audience. It is the constant drip, drip of connection in a world that can be isolating and unyielding. Compassion is more reactive, ignited by a problem or crisis; it is intense and more energy-draining. We can suffer from compassion-fatigue, but I haven't heard of kindness-collapse.

Leo Tolstoy drew on a lifetime of experience to write, 'The kinder and the more thoughtful a person is, the more kindness he can find in other people. Kindness enriches our life; with kindness mysterious things become clear, difficult things become easy, and dull things become cheerful.' In Kurt Vonnegut's book, *God Bless you Mr Rosewater*, the protagonist, Eliot Rosewater, baptizes twins by welcoming them to crowded Planet Earth and explains that there is only one rule to obey, 'God damn it, you've got to be kind.'

I feel the power of kindness walking between lockdowns, when the world is fearful and the road is empty. At the end of one long day, an old lady will see me trudging past her gate and will hand me fresh figs from her garden. She will then touch my face with a look of such tenderness it is hard to describe. A delightful Mexican couple will invite me to share their room in a hostel one bitterly cold night when there is nowhere else open and the only other option is the kitchen floor; the next day, they sing to me as we walk together. Early one morning, towards the end of the Camino, an old man brings over hot chocolate and churros to a park bench to share for breakfast, and we eat together in silence as the sun rises.

I can only imagine how much more intensely kindness is expressed when the road is filled with humanity on a quest for something that has goodness at its heart. The taxi driver who collected me from the stern doctor in Puente la Reina introduces herself as Maria. She offers to drive me around the town to show me some highlights.

A near life-sized, Y-shaped crucifix hangs in a softly-lit apse of the stark yet beautiful Iglesia del Crucifijo (Church of the Crucifix) on the edge of town. The Romanesque, twelfth-century building seems rooted and serene in the face of so much change. It sits right on the Camino and next to the River Robo, a tributary of the Arga. This morning, the main nave is in semi-darkness, making the glowing crucifix appear to stand proud of the wall. It is thought to have been presented to the town in the fourteenth century by German pilgrims who had carried it from their homeland to thank the townspeople for their hospitality and service towards travellers. A dejected, tortured Christ hangs from the wooden arms in disturbing realism, his pain, in some measure, comforting to the poor who often endured so much suffering in their daily lives. It is hard to look at a portrayal of agony and even harder to imagine the torment of the many who died from the brutal death sentence of crucifixion over the hundreds of years it was in use. It invites contemplation no matter who the observer or what their beliefs.

Maria and I sit for a while, wordless and wondering. The image goes beyond doctrine and religious division to address so many questions about what it means to be true to personal truth, no matter the consequences. This simple, austere yet warm church is a million miles away from the gold and glitter in Roncesvalles, and so many other Camino churches whose gilded interiors shine in the gloom. This wooden crucifix is a wretched symbol of degradation, humiliation and execution, capturing the moments just before death. It is an open-armed surrender to the cruel heart of humanity. The purpose of any piece of art is to summon the viewer to enter a story, to become immersed in its narrative, to ask questions, to search for answers, no matter how uncomfortable. As the fourteenth-century Dominican theologian Fra Giordano da Pisa stressed, art can only be truly appreciated if it is seen with a layered vision – involving the visual eye, the mind's eye and the soul. This depiction of a dying Christ shows him at the very point where even God himself experienced doubt, hanging on 'the shoreline of mystery', to steal a phrase from the late American art critic, Peter Schjeldahl:

Looking at art is like, 'Here are the answers. What were the questions?' I think of it like espionage, 'walking the cat back' – why did that happen, and that? – and eventually you come to a point of irreducible mystery. With ninety percent of work the inquiry breaks down very quickly. You reach an explanation that

is comprehensive and boring. Bad art, as any good artist will tell
you, is the most instructive, because it's naked in its decisions.
Even adorably so. When something falls apart you can see what
it's made of. Whereas with a great artist, say Manet or
Shakespeare, you're left gawking like an idiot.

Religious art is valued by the atheist and philosopher
Alain de Botton, who is not so much interested in the
existence of God, but in understanding why religions exist
at all. What fundamental aspects of the human psyche are
they addressing? He starts with the assumption that we
have made up the supernatural, but then, he says, we should
move the conversation on. 'What can religions teach us
and provoke us with today?' De Botton believes atheism
can gain a deeper understanding of human needs and
desires by engaging with religion, not ignoring it. Religious
art, he argues, is never in any doubt about its purpose,
which is to teach us how to live, what to love and what to
fear. He points out that some of the greatest artistic
geniuses to have ever lived have put their minds and talents
to depicting these precepts, why wouldn't we want to
know what they have to say? The universals of goodness,
kindness, truthfulness, generosity, compassion as well as the
many negative sides of human nature, such as cruelty and
deceitfulness, are what religious art is about. De Botton
believes it can help anyone contemplating their own god-
filled or god-free lives. Look at Leonardo da Vinci's *Last*
Supper, he says, if you want a lesson in not being a cheat
and a liar, look at the many depictions of Mary with the
child Jesus to see tenderness, stare at a crucifixion scene if
you need a reminder of what pure courage looks like.

The pain in my infected foot seems more bearable as we
drive to the banks of the River Arga at the other end of

town, to see the elegant six-arched bridge from which the town gets its name. Built in the eleventh century on the orders of Queen Doña Mayor, the wife of Sancho III of Navarre, it is renowned throughout Europe for its construction. The queen was a fervent advocate for pilgrimage and wanted to put an end to the extortionate fees being charged by locals to ferry pilgrims across the river. Puente la Reina, the Queen's Bridge, is where water, stars, miracles and pilgrims meet. Legend tells of eleventh-century shepherds following shooting stars that led to a cave in the side of a hill near the town. Inside they found a statue of the virgin and child and it was put on display in an alcove on the bridge as a benediction to pilgrims on their way to Santiago. Locals noticed that every day a bird (species unidentified) came to brush cobwebs away with its wings and to scoop water in its beak from the river to clean the face of Mary. So regular were the visits over the years (presumably not by the same bird) that celebrations and festivals developed and became an attraction. No matter how big the crowds or how loudly the church bells tolled, a bird always arrived to clean the statue. The last documented visit was in 1843, the year the turrets on the bridge had fallen so badly into disrepair they were demolished. Mary was moved inside the church of San Pedro for safety, and the association with birds ended.

I am to come across other statues of the virgin and child found in secret places, even inside felled trees; miraculous discoveries scattered along the trail providing focal points for devotion. Inevitably, there is speculation about the marketing potential of miracles and statues, which still draw thousands to the Camino, but like the relics of saints, they say more about our desires than they do about documented facts.

I'm not sure what to make of the story of magical birds flitting around a miraculous statue nestled in the Valley of the Stars below the Hill of Forgiveness; it all seems as extraordinary as it is charming. As we drive on, Maria smiles and tells me that she is sure I will make it to Santiago, and when I do, would I pray for her and send her a text? She then says a word I have been waiting to hear – Ultreia.

Ultreia, a traditional pilgrim greeting that appears in the *Codex Calixtinus*, is derived from two Latin words, *ultra*, meaning on the far side of, or beyond the horizon, and *eia*, which is a kindly encouragement to 'walk further – to keep going.' Ultreia was a medieval fist-bump exchanged by people on the road, a medieval 'You got this!' It has overtones of determination and tenacity; a recognition of the effort being put in, and the significance of the journey's end. If I were ever to have a tattoo, I would choose Ultreia, and display it somewhere visible. We all need encouragement to carry on, recognition from friends and strangers that our journey is worthwhile, that the effort we put in will, in some way, be worth it. The city streets, the highways and the byways of the world would surely benefit if this greeting were still in everyday use.

Maria has settled my mind, I will sit out the infection. A haze of discomfort, nausea and daytime television dominate the next few days. The only available pro-grammes are Spanish chat shows or a rolling American news channel dedicated to finance and business. There is talk of a 'blue wave', in the expectation that Biden will win America's presidential election. It is hard to believe looking at the near hysteria into which an unmasked Trump can whip his crowds; the social-media demagogue stands as defiant and proud as an emperor, telling people he could kiss them all.

Covid dominates the news online, but scrolling down, fires in the Amazon rainforest in Brazil also vie for space. In October 2020, the Institute of Space Research recorded over 17,000 fires, compared to just under 8,000 in October the year before. Distressing pictures of scorched, smoking trees and lines of fire stretching to the distance are enough to make you weep. The reports also highlight an unprecedented number of fires in the Pantanal, a vast wetland region to the south of the Amazon; its horror brought into focus by a photograph of a rescued anteater in an animal sanctuary. It is lying on its side, attached to a drip, its badly burned body covered in bandages. Illegal deforestation in the Pantanal more than doubled in the first six months of 2020, made worse by the most severe drought for nearly fifty years.

Dried out forests increase the likelihood and severity of wildfires. Many are caused by people clearing the land then setting it alight to prepare for cattle grazing and mining. Some are poor farmers trying to make a living, others are large companies who defy the law because future profits will be much higher than any fines imposed. The flames that leap from the screen are fanned by a destructive economic system that gives no economic value to wildlife, with the result that countless mammals, birds, reptiles, insects and plant life are allowed to perish.

For the far-right, populist president of Brazil, Jair Bolsonaro, the rich wilderness areas of the Amazon and the Pantanal are cash cows. After he took office in 2019, deforestation in the Amazon increased by 25 per cent during 2020, and a further 22 per cent in 2021. 'You have to understand the Amazon is Brazil's, not yours,' he said at a press conference in 2019, dismissing the wildfire data as a lie and alarmist. If forests and wetlands are to be protected, Bolsonaro wants the rest of the world to pay for income foregone, after all, he rails, 'you destroyed your own ecosystems.'

In 2018, Pope Francis visited the Amazon. Ninety-nine per cent of the rainforest lies within Catholic countries. 'The sky is angry,' he said, 'and is crying because we are destroying the planet.' Indeed, many people too are weeping with anger, fear and helplessness. This great forest of 55 million km^2 helps to regulate the world's climate, its rivers provide one-third of the fresh water entering the oceans, and the whole forest is a living, breathing temple to biodiversity. The Catholic Church, which has an immense influence over the whole Amazonian basin, has a moral duty to speak truth to power. Only a formidable alliance between politicians, local peoples, concerned citizens, green economists, conservationists, the media, the law, and a worldwide, powerful religion can stop the destruction.

And then, there is Australia. Between November 2019 and February 2020, this vast and extraordinary continent starts to burn. A report from the World Wildlife Fund (WWF) in Australia brings the magnitude of the disaster to the world's attention. Wildfires destroy up to 338,000 km^2 of land and over 30 people die. Millions of creatures are either killed or badly affected by injury or the loss of habitat, including 63,000 koalas, 5 million kangaroos and wallabies, 5 million bats, and 39 million possums. It is estimated that 2.46 billion reptiles and 181 million birds were in the path of the flames. Dermot Gorman, the chief executive of WWF Australia, says that as a wildlife disaster, it is one of the worst in modern history. The devastation doesn't remain on the continent. Satellite images show red smoke from the fires drifting eastwards over the Southern Ocean. Vast algal blooms are triggered by the ash thousands of miles away, which are 'larger than

Australia itself'. It also put vast amounts of CO_2 into the atmosphere. A report published online in *Nature* outlines the findings of meteorologist Ivar van der Velde. The emissions, he claims, 'from this single event were significantly higher than what all Australians normally emit with the combustion of fossil fuels in an entire year'.

An Australian artist friend, Janno Mclaughlin, painted a series of brightly coloured yet desperate works to depict the pain she saw all around her home in New South Wales. 'As koalas screamed in the background, the farmer cried as he shot all his cattle, they were in so much pain from burns inside and out,' she wrote on Facebook™, next to her painting of kangaroos, koalas, cockatoos, parrots and magpies tumbling through a pink sky above a burning forest.

2020 sees an acceleration of assaults on the wild lands of the world, and the stresses are heightened by a warming Earth. A blog written by NASA's Earth Observing System reports some of the major incidents. The United States Forest Service reports a 78-day increase in fires in California and Colorado, when California alone lost four million acres of forest in over 9,000 fires. In early October, an oil spill in Kamchatka in Russia saw tens of thousands of gallons of oil smother precious wildlife habitat, killing 95 per cent of wildlife on the seabed and triggering a declaration of a state of emergency. Satellite imagery highlights deepening and lengthening cracks in the Antarctic ice shelf, indicating that a major calving event is imminent. A few months later, in February 2021, a 1,270km² iceberg breaks away. In July 2020, one third of Bangladesh was submerged after heavy rainfall, and 550 people lose their lives. Closer to home in the United Kingdom, February 2020 was the wettest on record. High rainfall and Atlantic storms caused widespread flooding; in four months, almost 5,000 homes are inundated with water.

From my vantage point in a small, ancient Spanish town in October 2020, the world is diseased, drenched, choking, poisoned and burning. A blackened single tree surrounded by smouldering devastation and the distressing footage of an orangutan trying to fight off a bulldozer that is threatening its home offer further damning testimony of our heartlessness. This year of pain and reckoning is transmitted to me on the Camino through the small screen of a smartphone. Staring, despairing eyes – human and non-human – force questions, demand answers, but none are forthcoming. What can any one individual do in the face of this enormity?

In 2014, Jane Hirschfield wrote 'Let Them Not Say', a poem that imagines the young of tomorrow looking back on today. It is a moving plea to act so that future generations don't despair at what we allowed to go unchallenged on our watch – we heard, we saw, we witnessed, and we understood, yet we failed. 'Let them not say: they did nothing. We did not enough.'

When interviewed about it, Hirschfield said that she hoped it would not come true. Only a few years later, we live on a desperate planet laid low by a virus and beset by environmental crises brought about by our own actions.

On the way back, Maria and I drive past people queuing outside an open doorway in the main street, which leads into what looks like a workshop. Red peppers hang from strings on the outside walls, a painterly scene of scarlet bunches against sandy stone. Just inside the door are stacked crates of red bell-peppers, and a furnace glows brightly in the gloom. An acrid, bittersweet smell of vegetables, charcoal and carbon drifts through the air.

People are leaving the workshop carrying bulging, steaming plastic bags of the local speciality, roasted red peppers, and this is the height of the season. Every autumn people converge on the town from miles around, making Puente la Reina the roasted pepper capital of Spain. A market by the main church is red pepper central. Different farms have their own stalls, peppers are poured in through an opening at the top and black-skinned, steaming peppers emerge from a chute at the other end. Lines of people sit on the margins of the market stalls de-coring boxes of peppers, ready for roasting. Despite Covid it is bustling and getting busier. The church bells chime across a wonderful, peppery scene. Pedro, the owner of the hotel who has lived his whole life in Puente la Reina, offers to take me to see where the peppers grow. What follows is an unforgettable afternoon of modern economic migration, murder and mystery.

Pedro hums constantly as we drive to the outskirts of town. We communicate mainly through Google Translate™; trying to understand Spanish is difficult enough, through a mask it is impossible. I am told that there were no pilgrims in the town 30 years ago; 'pilgrim' was just a word Pedro had heard associated with the bridge. Then, 20 years ago, it took off, he thinks in part due to the film *The Way*, which boosted a growing rediscovery of pilgrimage to counter an increasingly unhappy world. Now pilgrims provide the bulk of his income and he is doing very well. The government promotes the route too, pilgrimage is guaranteed tourist money. Cordis, a community research and development organisation, studied the economic impact of the Camino in 2019 and estimated that it exceeded €300 million. Although hundreds of thousands of people walk the Camino annually, only 4 per cent of them describe themselves as tourists, preferring the term pilgrim, but the money is welcome no matter who spends it. Such an influx of people over a relatively short period must be overwhelming, and I ask Pedro if he welcomes the constant stream of people who now pass through his door? He nods sincerely and tells me he can never repay the richness they bring, spiritually and economically. Apparently, the English have even inspired a saying, 'You are heavier than an English pilgrim!' Meaning someone is overstaying their welcome. I'm not sure what to make of that.

Lines of red bell-pepper plants cover the undulating hills surrounding the town. This is such pleasing country, the last ripples of the Pyrenees provide soft, rolling farmland, rich red and sky blue. A few farmers walk the lines of their crops, and they wave as we drive past. In one large field, around eight men are busy at work, hunched and sweating as they throw peppers into large baskets. Pedro winds down the window and speaks to the supervisor; they laugh and exchange news, but when I ask if I can take a photograph, he shakes his head. It is only then that I notice most of the men have turned their backs and are shielding their faces with scarves. These are illegal workers from Morocco. Nearly 4,000 illegal Moroccan immigrants made the dangerous journey over land and sea in 2020, which was only a small percentage of the 41,000 economic migrants who arrived without papers or legal status.

With only 13km of sea separating Spain from North Africa, and given the country's close ties to South America, Spain is the chosen destination for a significant number of people seeking a better life in Europe. The town of Ceuta, a Spanish enclave in North Africa, has seen a dramatic increase in people trying to gain entry in recent years, and increasing incidents of violence along its borders. Strict laws deterring illegal crossings over the Mediterranean Sea have pushed migrant routes towards the Atlantic, making the Spanish-owned Canary Islands one of the main destinations for entry into Spain. Statista recorded 637 deaths by drowning in 2020. Crowded, hellish and with a high chance of failure, none but the most desperate would take the risk. For those that do succeed, Navarre welcomes farm labour, like the men picking peppers before me. These are the ones living the dream, many thousands more keep trying to find a way.

On the whole, Spain has a long tradition of accepting different peoples to its shores. Perhaps as a reaction to the Franco era, for many years it lacked the far-right agenda, which is an increasing presence in so many other European countries. This is now changing. In 2013, the VOX party emerged into the mainstream and is described as 'radical right-wing'. It takes a strong anti-immigration stance and has called for the expulsion of tens of thousands of Muslims from Spain. It publicly supported Donald Trump's re-election campaign and is opposed to environmental protection, calling it a 'green religion'. As recently as April 2021, VOX voted against Spain's Law for Climate Change and Energy Transition, which passed despite the right-wing opposition. It also supports the continuation of bullfighting as a valued tradition and believes in the rights of citizens to keep guns in their homes. In 2017, the party had just over 2,000 members; in 2020 it was 17,253. By March 2022, VOX broke through and became part of the regional government of Castile y León, the next province I will walk through.

Just a stone's throw from the main Camino path, the twenty-first-century agendas of economic migration, emerging right-wing politics and the shifting ideological landscape of Europe are being played out amongst the red peppers of Navarre.

Pedro's tour cuts through low green hills, which create a string of delightful valleys. He points to a tiny chapel hunkered on a crest, breaking the skyline. Known as the hermitage of Arnotegui, it is an isolated, simple building which carries the stoicism of one who accepts the punishment of being banished to the margins. He tells me that in the fourteenth century, William (Guillaume), Duke of Aquitaine, spent his days in service, solitude and prayer in that rough-hewn chapel on a hill, begging forgiveness for murder. A story of violence and redemption is as old as the hills and this one is known as the Mystery of Obanos, the name of a nearby town. Princess Felicia, the sister of William, was sent on pilgrimage to Santiago de Compostela by her father ahead of an arranged marriage. She was so moved by the experience she decided to stay in Obanos and live as a nun, renouncing her high-born status and her suitor. Furious, her father sent William to bring her back, but when she refused, he stabbed her through the heart in a fit of rage. Overcome with remorse he made his own pilgrimage to the bones of St James and then returned to build this hermitage on the outskirts of the town. His life was spent in prayerful penitence, healing the sick and providing shelter for the weary. As different pilgrimage routes meet here, his services were always in demand. Both Felicia and William are revered as saints, and according to the guidebooks, when William's body was exhumed centuries after his death, a silver pilgrim's shell was found amongst his bones. Bizarrely, though, his skull was separated from the rest of his body and can be found encased in silver in the San Juan Bautista Church in Obanos. This story is commemorated biannually in Obanos in the play, *Misterio de Obanos*.

On one Camino forum, a traveller, Rebekah Scott, gives more detail about the rather one-sided commemoration of this sad tale:

> What's even wilder is the church in Obanos has his head (his body is buried at the monastery up on the hill). The head is inside a very fancy, head-size reliquary carved with his supposed features. There's an opening on the top, and a little tap at the bottom. A local guy told me the confraternity dedicated to the saint used to celebrate his feast day by pouring a jug of wine in the top, and sharing out the drinks poured from the bottom! Shock!

Nothing much is said of his courageous, murdered sister other than if people pray at her grave in Labiano, they will be cured of headaches.

How strange is this road, how many tales of the bizarre, the disturbing and the downright unsavoury, and how infuriating that women are so often diminished and marginalized.

At the end of the afternoon, we pull into a parking area and it takes me a while to realise where we are. But there, right in front of me is the church I thought I had missed when blisters stopped play, the one I had been longing to visit – the evocative, beguiling, Iglesia de Santa Maria de Eunate (St Mary of Eunate). It sits away from the town as a solitary and mysterious outpost amongst fields. Thought to be as old as the twelfth century, its octagonal design is based on the Church of the Holy Sepulchre in Jerusalem. The base of the building is fringed by 33 arches supported by pillars whose chapiters are covered in carvings of human faces, animals and monsters. It may once have been a cloister, but no one knows for sure. A belfry once served as both a watchtower and a beacon to guide pilgrims to the safety of its walls.

Red stone against a deep blue sky punches through the green, flat surroundings. I long to go inside, but Covid had closed these doors too. Archaeological digs nearby have revealed many bodies buried with the pilgrim's shell, suggesting it was once a place that ministered to the dying. Perhaps it was run by the infamous Knights Templar or the order known as the Knights Hospitaller, both old Catholic military orders that originated in Jerusalem, but there is no direct evidence. Today it still provides a place for goodness and is used by various charitable organisations and as a pilgrimage destination. More questions than answers swirl around its walls, but Eunate defies categorisation and remains shtum about its history.

The church in a flat field is undoubtedly special. To me, it was made for silence and peace, a house of prayer surrounded by crops and resonating with birdsong, tinged with an edge of mystery. With a backdrop of distant mountains and a canopy of stars, it is a calming and serene shrine to nature and to God. Echoes of the architecture of Jerusalem deepen the enigma, connecting the great pilgrimage in Spain with the ancient route to the Holy Land. Alone and holding fast to their purpose, buildings such as these are islands of mystery, they draw us to them, not to reveal their secrets but to speak of our limitations. Despite our cleverness, our ability to dig, unearth and analyse, there are some places that simply refuse to yield. They belong to another time, another mindset, a lost era. Time folds its wings around all dreams, no matter how fervently they are pursued.

Diary entry: St Felix's Church, North Norfolk, January 2022

A strong wind came off the North Sea and gulls blew across the Norfolk sky. After several days of rain, the world danced and shone, enlivened by bright sunlight.

Everywhere, the eye fell on flat fields of stunted crops, tugged by the wind. Rising out of the earth on the Sandringham Estate was the broken outline of St Felix's church, a jagged, decaying skeleton, part vegetation, part stone. Melancholic, ivy-clad and lonely, it was a sad sight, even on a sunny day. The church cast a long shadow, an unloved monument to a long-forgotten saint. Beyond the ruin, the land slopes to the vestige of a wetland, a relic of a marsh that once bridged land and sea. Vast tracts of reeds and channels of slow-moving water would once have been filled with bird calls and the whistle of the wind, but now everything has been drained and planted; only a patch of wet ground remains at the lowest point. Spent shotgun cartridges were scattered through the crops, as were a few old cans and chocolate wrappers. Maybe the shooters were after hares; one had bounded down the field as I approached. Standing beneath the tower and looking out to the land all around, it wasn't hard to conjure a time before guns and crops, to when this place resounded only to the cries of waterbirds and the splashing of the creatures of torpid flows. Just a little extra imagination, and it is possible to hear a half-drowned body being dragged to dry ground.

Legend has it that in the seventh century, St Felix sailed here from France to evangelise to the tribes of East Anglia and to save them from what the Venerable Bede called, 'long-standing unrighteousness and unhappiness'. Felix vowed that where he landed he would build a church. As he sailed through the channels a violent storm wrecked his boat. Felix would have perished save for a family of beavers who held him aloft on their backs and ferried him to the safety of higher ground, which is where he kept his promise and built a church. In a dotty addition to this fantastic tale, it is said that St Felix was so grateful to the beavers that he made one of them a bishop. The original church is long gone, replaced in the fourteenth century by a sturdier structure, which served the village of Babingley until the nineteenth century, when it was eventually abandoned. Left to fend for itself it quickly fell into ruin. The footprint of the old village is now covered in crops, and just a few houses remain on the main road nearby, but memories of its bizarre foundation are kept alive on the village sign, which shows a mitred beaver ministering to other beavers who sit in homage at its feet.

The overwhelming air of this ruin was stoicism in the face of decay. The square tower stood proud against the wind, its empty windows were eyes staring to the horizon as though contemplating its end. Jackdaws circled above, moving between the bare trees and the turrets, calling and fussing at the intrusion. Time has not spared this once fervent place of hope. It will undoubtedly sink into oblivion at some point, returning to the earth to be forgotten, and it will take with it the magical association of holy beavers in a dank marsh on a howling night of disaster and salvation. Today, though, the ruined church shares some of the peace of Eunate, though with a far greater air of melancholy and loss.

After a few days, I am on the road again. Being forced to stop was not the disaster I had feared. The days of healing turned into some of the most memorable I encountered. The fringes of the Camino, which most never see, and the days of enforced rest gave time for reflection on the soft-bodiedness of pilgrimage, the reality of our thin skins pitched against miles of hard roads. They are good lessons in humility. It deepens my admiration for those who made this long journey before the miracle of antibiotics and the benefit of soft beds, waterproof clothing and nourishing food. I will remember Puente la Reina with more clarity than many of the other days spent walking along roads with barely a glance to the world on the margins.

CHAPTER SIX

Wine and Wonder

Kindness pours onto the Camino, and wine flows outwards to fill the wine cellars of the world. The rolling hills between Puente la Reina and the magnificent cathedral city of Burgos, 200km away, are dedicated to grapes and wineries, interspersed with grey/green groves of olive trees. The *Codex Calixtinus* praises this region, 'where bread is good, wine excellent, meat and fish are abundant and which overflows with all delights'. The author, Aymeric Picaud, was obviously very glad to leave the mountains of the Pyrenees behind and enter this bountiful land.

The trail winds through vineyards producing the delicate rosé wines of Navarre and the aromatic, spicy reds of the Rioja region. Rows of vines stretch into the distance and hoop over the crests of the hills, they look like ribs standing proud of the earth. Tempting bunches of grapes are easily within reach; it is impossible not to taste the occasional one. Winemaking has been part of this land for centuries and vines flourish on the sand and clay soils, the gentle slopes, the sunlight and the waters taken from the rivers Alhama, Cidacos, Ebro, Oja and Tirón. The great monasteries that developed along the Camino became renowned vintners, developing wine for trade, pilgrims and for the sacraments. Red wine, after all, flows like blood through Christian culture. So important to trade and prosperity was the wine of the Rioja region it is said that in 1635, the capital city of the region, Logroño, prohibited carts from passing through the streets in case the vibrations affected the quality of the wines ageing in their barrels.

A glass of wine oils the wheels of conversation. So many souls gather on this line through the land and each one has a unique story to tell. The physical Camino is the skeleton, the bare bones on which to hang the flesh of a tale. The villages, towns and cities, the mountains, forests, wine regions, agricultural plains and upland farms form the universal chapter headings, the same story arc of a walk of 500 miles across northern Spain, but innumerable different adventures emerge. Each journey comprises a unique set of characters with an intricate, infinite web of back stories. It is this particularity that makes the Camino live in a million different hearts in a million different ways, and all of them begin by walking.

When people say it is the journeying involved in pilgrimage that matters as much as the destination, it is because the time spent en route is the creative space that allows the invisible to get to work. The combination of walking, someone's personal history and the stories both old and new that are ever-present, all form a potent solution where feelings, hunches and notions begin to crystalise. They fill the void normally crowded out with daily life, getting stronger and more substantial as each day passes. It cannot be instantaneous, it is an unfolding, developing process, like mother of pearl accreting around a stone. Insight is born in the gap between experiencing and recognition, between an inkling and an understanding. Call it prayer if you like. Back home when it is all over, perhaps even years later, our brains analyse, dissect, sift and sort, and turn a raw experience into something containable, but before that, there are only beginnings, and they are unique.

The Japanese have a word for the potency of gaps, *Ma*, the space that defines the solid either side. Alan Fletcher's book on graphic design, *The Art of Looking Sidewards*, believes there is no creative expression without it. It is the meaning in gaps left in Henry Moore's contorted figures. He cites Cézanne as painting space to define reality, and the sculptor Giacometti as sculpting by 'taking the fat off space'. The actor Ralph Richardson believed that the power of acting lay in pauses, and music, said Isaac Stern, is the gap between notes, 'silences which give the form'. In Japanese, *manuke* means a fool, literally translated as someone who is missing *ma*, a person who cannot live in the gaps, an empty vessel which fills a space with the most noise. Everyone on the road is caught up in this process of formation in their own way. Our everyday lives are overwhelmed by practicalities and the drama of our news-driven, social-media-skewed world. Only what makes it into the spotlight gets our attention. It is too easy to forget the importance of the shadowy things, the secretive and half-buried, and the fact that they take time to find, and that the seeking is part of the process. I meet very few people on the trail, but those I do are in the middle of opening their hearts and minds to these quieter offshoots of the mainstream.

In a half-empty restaurant one evening I eat at the same table as Pierre, a young Frenchman who is travelling alone after leaving the army. He set out from Mont St Michel in Normandy and has already completed 800km and still has 600km to go. He is tall, wiry and well-ordered, although after so long on the road his red hair is straggly and his beard growing longer and more unkempt. Dressed in a rough-hewn cloak, with a staff and a gourd, he could well have walked out of the Middle Ages. His mission is well defined: to discern what he is destined to do and to be. Should he marry his girlfriend, train as a maths teacher and settle into conventional coupledom, or leave his lover and live a solitary, contemplative life away from normal expectations? He tells me he is travelling with the blessing of his partner, who loves him enough to let him go if that is what he decides to do. With the intensity of someone driven by an inner quest, he possesses a quiet strength. He says grace before eating his food, which is plain and sparse with no dessert, and his accommodation is the cheapest available. On most days he covers a full 40km, twice as far as I often manage, no doubt the army has instilled fortitude and stamina. As he leaves I wish him well, he takes with him my admiration; few in their late twenties possess his singularity and self-understanding. I certainly didn't, and I don't doubt he will find the right path.

Further along the Camino, I meet four men who had been brought together through serendipity, two Italians, a Canadian and an American. All four are making decisions, choosing between well-worn tracks and less-certain roads. One of the Italians works as a sailor on tourist yachts in Sorrento. The clients are often demanding and rude, and he longs to break free from a life based on serving the rich; even though he loves the sea and boats, it is not enough. How to make the break, though, is unclear. His friend has many different jobs, but none are satisfying. He is treading water when there is an ocean of experience to explore as an artist. Simply by talking about art his demeanour changes. He is handsome and outwardly self-assured, but his eyes hold pain from a difficult relationship with his father, who suffers from depression. The Canadian has a degree in engineering, but he wants a career writing fantasy and science-fiction novels. He is nervous of leaving a life of well-paid certainty for the hard graft of an unknown author. The American is older and a lay Franciscan (men and women who live in the spirit of St Francis without taking holy orders). He is a deeply spiritual man who loves animals, loves God and is on his

way to meet his boyfriend in Santiago. He is searching for
the next step but seems like a bird flying in a strong wind
and finding it hard to keep course, buffeted by forces he
can't control. All four are fun and generous, sharing their
laughter and thoughts freely with me over an evening
meal. It is too easy to trot out pithy sayings – go with
your heart, be true to yourself, follow the road less
travelled – platitudes that are as thin and as brittle as
antique glass; they add nothing and help no one. The
Camino does the talking. What feels corny in conversation
is poignant food for thought on the road. On a nearby
underpass covered in graffiti someone has written the
famous idiom, 'Love many, trust few, always paddle your
own canoe.' Perhaps they saw it too and are in the process
of interpreting it in the way they see fit.

The Jesuits have a name for the process of searching for
the right decision: 'discernment'. The right path will
materialise through meditating on the choices to be made
and then noticing shifts in interior energy, in what
promotes lightness and positivity and what feels heavy.
Discernment is a way of finding the rightness of a decision
based on an examination of inner motivations, so that
whatever is chosen comes from a place of goodness, not
of superficial happiness or popular opinion; settle for
anything less and the rocky road ahead may be too much
to bear.

Important decisions are just one motivation for taking
to the road, but there are many others. Addressing a
restlessness that won't be quietened is a powerful driver,
and the one I relate to the most. A chatty, funny Mexican
couple always make me smile whenever we meet. They
first catch me up, staring into the sky watching Griffon
vultures soaring on thermals. Their love of domestic
animals, especially dogs, means their small flat in Mexico

City houses a Great Dane, a pit bull, and two other dogs of mixed breed, all of them rescued from shelters. Angela had walked part of the Camino when she was single, but the experience was too vivid, heightened by hallucinations and nightmares. It was so disturbing for her, she gave up. She and her husband are now walking the 500 miles together, but this time she is wrapped in his supportive love. Christian's calm devotion counterbalances her big-hearted intensity and restlessness. Their shared Catholicism draws them into cathedrals and churches, into conversations deep into the night, and it keeps them laughing and singing all the way to Finisterre. I ask if they like living in Mexico City, reputed to be one of the most crime-ridden cities in the world, blighted by drug trafficking and corruption. No, they say, they would love to leave as soon as possible because life is stressful in a crowded city where trust is low and anxiety high, where anything can happen at any moment. It might go some way to explaining Angela's anxiousness. In her husband she has found a home for her heart, but her soul is yet to find a peaceful harbour.

And then there are those pilgrims who are drawn to the deep comfort of the Camino, to an ancient certainty that has been tried and tested over generations. These are the so-called 'Camino Orphans', people whose lives only make sense on the trail. Some spend years on it, living in albergues and exchanging labour for free accommodation. The Camino gathers them in. James is one such troubled soul, a young Englishman in his twenties. I meet him as I take refuge for the night in a brand new albergue on the outskirts of Arzúa, a city towards the end of the Camino. It has been another day of heavy rain and wind. I stand in the doorway, dripping, soaked to the skin and badly in need of warmth. He is the only person in the building. He makes me tea and puts biscuits on a plate, shows me to an empty dormitory and offers to put my wet clothes in the dryer. We then sit together as night falls and sheets of rain batter the street. James is estranged from both of his divorced parents; his mother has remarried and doesn't want him around and his father is ill and can't support him. He has no siblings, no obvious place to call home, nowhere he feels welcome, no job to return to, no connections to draw him back; he is washed up and alone in a pilgrim hostel on a busy and faceless main road in Spain. Caught in an eddy, going round and round in his head, he is unable to go forwards or backwards, unable to break free. The albergue owner is kind and allows him to stay at a reduced rate in exchange for some simple duties, but James' savings are running out. He has made a home of sorts in a small room on the ground floor by the communal kitchen which is never used, and everything he possesses fits into a rucksack. He told me no one has stayed in the albergue for weeks, and that he is glad of company, especially for the chance to speak English. James had spent days following the Camino Portuguese, walking on his own, and had not met anyone else. Negative thoughts and the intense loneliness became unbearable; he knew he was sinking. Arzúa is a point of confluence where other routes join the main Camino Francés for the last few days to Santiago, and here at least there is more chance of meeting people. He desperately needs company. He tells me he wants some kind of sign or flash of inspiration to make it clear where he should go next, but there has been no one to explore ideas with, no one to listen.

We talk for a long time that night. Outside, the streetlights highlight near-horizontal rain, inside, bright white strip lights illuminate a brand-new hostel empty of all but two guests. Rain pounds the large glass windows that front onto the street and bounces off the pavement; rivers of water run down the gutters and the cars send sprays of water into the air. It is a fitting underscore to James' story of a life of anxiety and depression and his longing for love and security. He tells me he met a Japanese woman a while ago and they exchanged addresses; he thought he might go to Japan to find her, but he wasn't sure she would want to see him. I offer some suggestions for finding work online to help keep him going financially, and it seems that anyone taking an interest in his life is welcome. His soul is troubled but his heart is kind, and James has so much more to offer than to be a Camino refugee. He represents the many who become untethered from a secure life and find some kind of purpose on an ancient trackway. The Way of St James attracts the lost, the vulnerable and those looking for love, searching for a path to keep them on the rails and to guide them to a safe haven. For James, the Camino is a home as well as a journey.

The next morning, I take him for breakfast in a café downtown, which he devours. Money is limited to just a few euros a day and his diet is sparse. He then walks with me to where the track leaves the city and veers off into fields; he is still waving goodbye as I turn a corner and out of sight.

It is a very modern undertaking to go on pilgrimage to search within for answers to life's questions. For much of human history, especially in the West, those answers were found in the realm of an external deity; the meaning of life was framed within prescribed Christian doctrine. A medieval pilgrimage fell within particular bounds: to honour the saints, to offer service to God, to seek forgiveness for grievous sin (murder was a common one), to gain indulgences (a way to reduce the punishment for sins in the afterlife) and to ask for healing from sickness. The idea of pilgrimage to explore your inner landscape would have made no sense. As the centuries have rolled by, individualism has trumped the once unassailable role of religion. Conformity to doctrine has given way to autonomy, and, in the West in particular, belonging to an organised religion is far less common than ascribing to a more diffuse spirituality. What hasn't changed is the search for a higher connection, which is as important as it ever was. And much of the sharing of the journey is done over food and drink in the evening.

In the past, wine had a practical side too; wine, cider or beer were often safer to drink than the local water supply. But for a thirsty and probably dehydrated pilgrim, drinking alcohol was dangerous; intoxicated travellers were easily swindled. The 'Veneranda Dies', a long sermon in Book I of the *Codex Calixtinus*, describes, with barely contained fury, the many crimes devout pilgrims had to suffer at the hands of the wily locals. They include innkeepers who would allow a pilgrim to sample the best wine, but then fill their glass with the cheapest, maybe even stooping as low as to mix it with cider. They would cover water fountains so that travellers were forced to buy wine and then wait until they were drunk and steal their belongings to sell at inflated prices. Some sold food that was days old, or they used trick measuring cups to make a purchase look bigger than it was. The sale of sub-standard candles was also rife. If a pilgrim survived disease, natural dangers and the physical demands of travelling, they would still have to contend with the malfeasance of the locals.

A long road through vineyards and olive groves leads to the medieval hilltop village of Cirauqui, a few kilometres

on from Puente la Reina. It is a beautiful sight as it comes
into view, perfectly circular and contained, as though
someone had used a compass to draw around the crest of
the hill and nothing was allowed to be built beyond the
line. The russet-red track and orange soil of the fields glow
in the sunshine. A lone olive tree growing on a verge and
rows of vines mark the climb to the entrance of the village.
Curiously, the ancient name 'Cirauqui' translates as 'nest of
vipers', which is incongruous for such a pretty setting.
Some interpretations reference the snakes that once lived
in the walls along the river; others think the name has
more to do with the tricks that were inflicted on the poor,
hungover pilgrims who had no option but to follow the
trail. A bridge crosses over a tributary of the Rio Salado
(or Salt River) just beyond the village and it is here,
according to a personal account in the *Calixtinus*, the
unwary could easily fall victim to foul play:

> *Beware from drinking its waters or from watering your horse in
> its stream, for this river is deadly. While we were proceeding
> towards Santiago, we found two Navarrese seated on its banks
> and sharpening their knives; they make a habit of skinning the
> mounts of the pilgrims that drink from the river and die. To our
> questions they answered with a lie, saying that the water was
> indeed healthy and drinkable. Accordingly, we watered our horses
> in the stream, and had no sooner done so, than two of them died:
> these the men skinned on the spot.*

In fact, this medieval travel guide warns of deadly
poisonings for people as well as animals. It lists the different
rivers and the fish that must be avoided in Navarre,
particularly it warns against eating barbel, tench and eels,
advising, 'Should you eat any of them in any part of Spain
or Galicia, you will undoubtedly die shortly afterwards or

at least fall ill.' There is some truth in the barbel advice. Barbel eggs (or roe), but not the flesh, are poisonous to people, so much so the condition is referred to as 'barbel cholera'. Eel blood is likewise extremely poisonous if eaten raw. The inclusion of tench is a mystery, especially so as it was considered a 'doctor fish'. The particularly thick slime covering its body was thought to heal other fish that rubbed up against it, causing some people to boil the slime and use it as an ointment. Some doctors recommended tying a live tench to the stomach to cure jaundice or advised strapping one around your head to get rid of headaches or to the back of the neck for eye inflammation. Surprisingly, if one was tied onto the soles of the feet, it was thought to cure the plague and reduce fever.

The perils faced by pilgrims over the ages were varied and real. No wonder amulets, badges or other trinkets were carried on the journey to ward off evil, both natural and human. If these were held against a shrine it was thought their power could be recharged by a holy flow of energy. One of the likely reasons for wearing the badges depicting genitalia was to repel death by sporting images of what gives life. Some travellers carried certain gems that were thought to have special powers; for the wealthy, emeralds, diamonds and rubies were especially popular. These were either sown onto clothing or dropped into drinks to neutralise poisons. One fabled cure was to carry a bezoar, a hardened spherical deposit of indigestible material that forms in the gastrointestinal tract of ungulates, but, unsurprisingly, they were not that easy to obtain. Another recommended method was to carry shavings from the horn of a unicorn (probably the tusk of a whale called a narwhal), which was, presumably, no less difficult to find.

Bizarre as they seem today, when faced with a world of dangers, both seen and unseen, any promise of protection was seized upon. Perhaps a pause for thought is worthwhile. Crystal healing and protection is alive and well and has enjoyed a revival in recent times. The Covid pandemic saw a steady increase in internet searches for 'crystal healing' and 'crystal shops near me'. The singer Adele believes crystals reduce her anxiety on stage and Gwyneth Paltrow's lifestyle brand offers a medicine bag complete with crystals to help with clarity of thought, serenity, courage, creativity and emotional strength. For around $100 you can buy water bottles with healing crystals built into the structure. Religions still hold to the power of relics and medals. A family member gave me a St Christopher medallion that had been blessed by a priest to carry with me for protection on my journey. How much more were these aids relied upon prior to the Enlightenment in the seventeenth and eighteenth centuries. Before the dominance of science, a person's soul, mind, intellect and emotions were thought to be intimately connected, playing off each other and affecting well-being. A healthy, harmonious state could only be the result of a balance between the different aspects of being human. Although it is less extreme today, we are seeing a movement back to this idea in some areas of modern medicine. If you believe something will do you good, often it will have a beneficial effect. If you are told something will help you, while it may not actually be a cure, there is some suggestion that it hastens recovery.

In the end, though, no number of medals or crystals will be sufficient; we all succumb and are rendered up to time. A sign over the cemetery at the town of Los Arcos (the arches) a little further along the trail reads, 'You are what I once was, and will be what I am now.'

Today, water from the many drinking fountains is clean and pure, but even in the daytime a glass of wine is welcome, and difficult to resist if it is free. 'If you want to go to Santiago with strength and vitality, of this great wine have a drink and toast to happiness,' reads the sign over one of the most famous stops on the whole Camino. On a wall of the ancient monastery and winery of Santa María de Irache is a drinking fountain with a difference. Out of one tap flows red wine, out of the other, potable water. It is a generous gift, but it is not always treated with respect. Below the sign wishing pilgrims a happy journey was another reminding people that even though 100 litres are provided each day, everyone should be restrained and leave enough for others: 'Unfortunately, we cannot provide a jug because of continuous burglaries.'

The Irache wine fountain is an obligatory place for photographs, and mine is taken by a middle-aged Englishman called Frank, one of the only two British people I speak to on the whole journey (James being the other). Frank has a different motivation for walking the Camino. As he sips wine out of a newly acquired scallop shell, he tells me that he is on a walking holiday. I comment on his shell's symbol of pilgrimage, which surprises him. He has no idea what I am talking about and seems to be unaware of the religious significance of the route. The thousand-years of religion and the bones of St James (who he has never heard of), are irrelevant, the end point, the cathedral at Santiago de Compostela, is a place to catch the bus to the airport. For Frank, the Camino is a line on a map, no different to any other walking route. He listens attentively to what little I tell him, but he says he isn't much interested in history, and definitely not religion; he just wants to cover as many miles each day as he can and to enjoy the scenery. Frank is a bullet train speeding through northern Spain, skimming over the surface, forward–facing and kilometre-focussed. He cuts through the landscape, resistant to the flavour and shape of all that has come together to make this track what it is. But it does not matter; his reasons for being at the Irache wine fountain are as valid as mine. Frank is proof that the Camino is multifaceted and multifunctional, a trail that welcomes everyone. It does not judge, it does not demand and it does not expect; it is there for whichever soul is drawn to walk its paths, and it gives in equal measure no matter what the motivation. Frank is pleasant company and we part at a divide in the road just a short distance ahead; he takes the shorter, traditional path along the valley and I opt for an alternative, higher road through forests and a range of hills.

The Camino often splits to offer two or more different routes that run roughly alongside each other, but cross and re-cross like braided lines. Usually, the one most followed is the main track, but there can be an option to walk quieter, more remote roads with fewer services. As I have everything I need for the day, and as there is so little open anyway, I opt for the one less travelled. It quickly gains height, and winds through forests and farmland to offer glorious views. The rich aroma of holm oak and pines and the sparse warbling of birds creates an atmosphere so magical that Bilbo Baggins and his company of dwarves would not be out of place here, singing and squabbling as they stride to their next adventure. Celtic mythology has druids, seers, teachers, astronomers and healers meeting together in the shelter of ancient holm oaks, and Zeus, the father of the Greek gods, was said to speak through the murmuring of its leaves. As it is evergreen, women wore holm oak acorns as amulets to help them get pregnant. The Virgin Mary appeared to a group of children, hovering above a holm oak in Fatima in Portugal, which is now a renowned pilgrimage destination.

For generations of Spanish farmers, the trees provided shade for animals, wood for fire, and the acorns were food for people and livestock. Holm oaks were once considered so integral to Spanish rural life that it was said they were as important to Spanish peasants as seals were to the Inuits. It is the oak wood that is so prized in wine-growing regions, providing the tight-grained, tannin-rich barrels for the storage and ageing of the wine.

Holm oaks are common throughout my home city of Bristol, where they were introduced from the Mediterranean a few centuries ago. A striking specimen sits in the middle of my local green space, a raised, grassy square enclosed by stone walls and surrounded by elegant Georgian housing. It looks solid and dependable, spreading its substantial crown over the lawn, and very little grows in its shade. Compared to the light, leafy warmth of an English oak, it is a cold and austere tree, but a fitting place-keeper for this particular spot. This was the site of a seventeenth century hill fort, Prior's Hill Fort, which was built to defend north Bristol during the English Civil War. It saw heavy fighting and much loss of life, and was eventually overrun, which proved to be a turning point. 'Without obtaining this fort all the rest of the line to Frome river would have done us little good; and indeed neither horse nor foot would have stood in all that way, in any manner of security, had not the fort been taken.' So said Oliver Cromwell in 1645, his words now on a plaque by the gate. The oak and the grassy square provide tranquillity, a breathing space in the city, and most people never think of the blood that was spilled here. Our complex history is played out on the same stretch of land, all of that war and violence absorbed into present-day gentility.

So too with the Camino. A ruined fort sits atop the strikingly conical peak of Monjardín, which dominates the

view from the Irache wine fountain to Los Arcos. It must
once have been a magnificent citadel, but now lies in ruins.
It was the last stronghold of the Moors in this region of
Spain, taken back by the Christian King Sancho García in
the tenth century, and it saw bitter bloodshed. On the
lower slopes of this historic mountain are the vines of the
Monjardín winery, the grapes of which are said to be
enhanced by the famed 'cierzo wind', a strong, dry, cold
airstream from the north-west, which blows most frequently
in autumn and winter. It can reach speeds of 100km an
hour and has been described since ancient times. In the
second century BC, Cato the Elder said its strength made it
difficult to breathe and it blew over wagons and fully-
armed men. Luckily, on this autumnal day it is a refreshing
and buffeting breeze rather than a flattening gale. The track
is well defined and the air enlivening. The feeling of peace
and tranquillity, perhaps aided by the Irache wine, is all-
pervasive. It feels good to be on the road again, and there is
nowhere on Earth I would rather be. As I leave the forest
for more open ground, the views are magnificent. To the
left, fields and woodland extend up the mountainside, to
the right, sloping meadows dotted with copses drop away
to the valley below. There, snaking through farmland is the
main Camino track, carrying Frank ever onwards.

I see no one on the trail, only a couple of cars parked
by a field gate, which I assume belong to hunters. The
wild boar season is well underway and occasional gunshots
resound somewhere in the distance. A sign on the footpath
warns of charging boar as beaters are driving the animals
towards the guns, but none appears, and no one is in sight.
I stop frequently to take photographs of the empty trail
curving ahead.

Eventually, the footpath descends to the small village of
Luquin, and a welcome rest. The communal square is

shady and drinking water flows from a fountain. I take out
the guidebook and look for my glasses. They are not in my
waist-belt or any pockets. After some panicked rummaging
I know, with a sinking feeling, that they have fallen out
somewhere along the trail; they could be anywhere. Tired
and cross, I retrace my steps back up to the hills. After
scouring the verges for an hour, especially around obvious
look-out spots, I'm not even sure I'm on the same path;
everything feels different walking in the opposite direction.
Other tracks appear that I hadn't noticed before, coming
in from the side or splitting off into fields and trees. The
grass is long, the way uncertain, and I still have a good
distance to cover before the end of the day. I give up and
head back to the village. After a grumpy half-hour's break,
I pick up the main trail towards the town of Los Arcos.
Before long, the Camino crosses the busy N-111, where
cars and lorries thunder by. Just as I run over the road, a car
brakes suddenly and pulls over. A Spanish woman steps out
and smiles, 'I think these are yours,' she says, handing me
my glasses. Just as quickly as she had arrived, she is gone,
leaving me dumbfounded, staring after her car.

Events like this raise questions about the nature of
coincidence. Even if she had been following me closely
enough to recognise me or to see my glasses fall, she
hadn't called out or caught me up, and I saw no one on
the trail, near or far. If she had found them later and
assumed someone looking like a walker was the likely
owner, it is amazing she happened to be driving down the
road at the same time as I was crossing it, quite a while
after the event. It remains one of those odd happenings,
but then this long and narrow road seems to be a draw for
so many things, from the mundane to the miraculous.

At the miraculous end, there is no shortage of bizarre
events that have supposedly taken place along the

Camino, most of them in the distant past. Their strangeness still draws people to ponder and to wonder. Would the Camino even exist without its litany of miracles? Although most people don't believe they are factual accounts of real events, there is still a fascination for the paranormal that hints beyond the human realm, happenings that we cannot fathom.

Nájera appears over a bridge, an ancient place with narrow streets that squeeze between the Rio Najerilla and towering cliffs of red sandstone pockmarked with man-made caves. Once the capital of the Navarre region, it is now a tourist attraction steeped in legend and bloodied history.

It is late afternoon, but the eleventh-century church-come-museum-come-mausoleum, Santa Maria la Real (Mary our Queen), is still open. A cold, quiet atmosphere seems particular to the resting place of the dead. My only companions are the serried ranks of the tombs of over two dozen kings who once reigned over Navarre; their dusty bones are all that remain of their earthly power and glory. One of them is García Sánchez III, who ruled this area in the eleventh century. It is said that García was tall, fit, blonde and handsome, and he loved to hunt. In 1044, his hawk chased a partridge into thick bushes on a hillside. Concerned when it didn't return, he fought his way through the vegetation and discovered an opening into the rock, one of the ancient caves excavated by hand thousands of years ago. Caves always have an open door; it is fear that is the barrier to going inside, but trepidation no doubt turned to astonishment when he found both the hawk and the partridge side by side beneath a rustic altar next to a lit lamp, a bell and a jug of white lilies. Above them was a statue of the virgin and child, glowing in the dark. As the king was locked in battle with the Moors, he took this as a sign and vowed to honour the statue with a church, and Santa Maria la Real is the result. It is built directly onto the cliff face and encompasses the cave.

The grand entrance surrounding the cave mouth is guarded by statues of King García and his queen, Estefanía, one on each side of the arched doorway. They are kneeling in prayer, staring to the horizon and lost in ecstasy. Stepping inside, I am as alone as García on that long-ago hunting trip when he suddenly found himself in darkness; a light-loving human surrounded by rock and dank air. Just ahead a smiling Mary and Jesus peer down from a ledge, glowing in soft lamplight. There is no one to share the looking, just me and an ancient wooden carving in as unlikely a setting as it is possible to imagine. The rich red, sandstone walls are bare and layered, with large white veins of quartz running through cracks in the rockface; the cavern remains as unadorned as when it was discovered. Mary is half life-size and sitting upright, her feet are apart and planted firmly on the ground, her shoes are pointed. She looks entirely comfortable, peasant-like, practical, earthy and very sweet. She could be a young mum in a mother and toddler group. Her almond-shaped face, high arched eyebrows, almond eyes and rosy cheeks above a pretty mouth give her a doll-like appearance. One hand is gently holding onto her baby sitting on one knee, the other holds what looks like a flower or globe. Her smile holds the indefinable emotions of the *Mona Lisa*, all-knowing, all-innocent and deeply at peace. Only her bejewelled coronet gives her away as the queen of heaven. In a strange connection to home, the original crown was stolen in the fourteenth century, and its precious stones divided up as spoils. Pedro the Cruel gave a particularly magnificent gemstone to Edward the Black Prince, and it now adorns the English coronation crown as the Black Prince Ruby.

Many things change over the lifetime of a human being, but not the darkness of caves. They do not bow to human clocks, there are no markers of day and night, just the slow drip-dripping of Earth time. Dungeons deep and caverns old are common in legends and myths. Their absence of light and echoey sound are disorientating. Their failure of presence, a blackness to be filled, means caves have always attracted and repelled us. All cultures, all religions, have given them special status. They are the entrance to the underworld, to the lairs of dragons and where the bones of giants are laid to rest; they are the dwelling place of light-loathing spirits. We go to caves to dream the dreams of different realities; where we hear voices and touch the other side. We have buried our dead and hidden treasures deep in their recesses, and painted, carved and whittled images inspired by their visions. They are where hermits found insights through meditation and self-denial, and where religious leaders received divine instruction. In Christian mythology, caves were also portals to hell, to that place of punishment where the damned are tortured forever, trapped in their misery with no one to hear them scream. No wonder, then, that Christianity wished them tamed. For medieval Christians, Mary and the Christ child brought goodness and order to these haunted spaces; they glowed with confidence in the chaos and confusion of the dark.

Christianity took power away from raw nature, it removed the spirit-filled natural world of ancient religions and replaced it with the gospel story. Peter Brown's book on the cult of saints in western Christianity wrote that a focus on the saints and the Holy Family resulted in, 'a natural world made passive by being shorn of the power of gods.' It is no surprise that the devout García is said to have found the statue in a cave, as did the peasants who found a similar one near Puente la Reina and placed it on the bridge into town. There are many other miraculous associations between Christianity and caves right across the Christian world; many of them are famous pilgrimage sites. One such is Lourdes in France, where a child is said to have seen multiple apparitions of Mary in a cave. The grotto now receives around 3.5 million pilgrims a year.

I love this pretty Madonna in a red cave, smiling sweetly through the gloom. The simplicity of the cavern adds to her gentle presence, and I mark her down as the kind of queen of heaven I prefer to the ornate, golden remote statues found in most other places. It is also a charming story. But then this region is renowned for its heart-warming and lovely tales that fold nature into its message.

The natural world and miracles are inextricably linked. A miracle bends nature's rules, a reminder that even the laws of the universe have an overlord. A few kilometres further down the trail from Nájera is the ancient town of Santo Domingo de la Calzada, St Domingo of the Causeway. Its name is derived from an eleventh-century holy man, St Domingo (or Dominic), who built bridges and maintained the trail, as well as a hospital to serve pilgrims. That is now an expensive hotel which forms one side of the town square, on the opposite side is the cathedral where one of the most endearing and whacky miracles of the whole pilgrimage is said to have been played out.

According to the *Codex Calixtinus*, a devout German family consisting of a mother, father and son called Hugonell, went on pilgrimage to Santiago. One evening at their lodgings, Hugonell caught the fancy of the innkeeper's daughter, who propositioned him. Being chaste and devout he turned her down and retreated to pray. Hell hath no fury *etc.*, so she took some silver from the local church and hid it inside Hugonell's bag. The next morning when the family went on their way, she cried foul and accused him of stealing. The hapless Hugonell was arrested, taken back to the town, tried in court, found guilty and hanged. When his heartbroken parents returned from Santiago, they went to the town to pray at their son's grave and were astonished to find him still hanging from the gallows in fine fettle. He told them it was St Domingo who had kept him alive at the end of the rope. His parents rushed to the judge to beg him to cut Hugonell down, but as the judge was just tucking into his evening meal of roast chicken and vegetables, and assuming they were mad with grief, he was in no mood to comply. He declared, 'Your son is as dead as the chicken on my plate!' Immediately, the roast meat sprouted feathers, sprung to life, and a cock and a hen ran around the room squawking and flapping. Nature's rules had most definitely been bent. They all ran to the gallows where they found Hugonell still hanging, still smiling and still administering blessings. The judge pardoned him, returned him to his parents and all was well. To this day, chickens (some say they are the direct descendants of the original roasted ones) sit in a gothic-style coop high up in a wall of the cathedral, pottering about in their brightly lit glass cage, well out of the reach of prodding and poking tourists; apparently, they are replaced every couple of weeks. Also displayed is a piece of the gallows.

Bizarre, delightful, audacious, ridiculous, comedic and rooted in justice, this story has all the elements needed for an enduring miraculous tale. It is told in frescoes and paintings on the walls around the cathedral, some with great detail. One mosaic shows Hugonell wearing a cloak with a scallop shell, and he is hanging from a rope; under his feet is the upturned stool that had been kicked away by the executioner. His large, dark eyes are serene, and his gaze follows you around the room. His hands are held out in benediction. On a table next to the gallows are two chickens standing on a dinner plate next to some vegetables, a knife and fork at the ready. The rooster has its head back and is in the middle of a full-throated cock-a-doodle-do. It is the oddest sight, and it makes me laugh out loud.

The chicken story is unique to St Domingo, as far as I know, but creaturely life is often drawn into the Christian story, as the hawk and partridge in Nájera also show. The chicken tale makes the point that even the humblest of creatures, hens that scratch around the yard, are channels of divine power, even when they are dead and roasted. Domesticated animals are usually considered the poor relations of wildlife, half-creatures that have been stripped of their cousins' wild dignity, the ones whose spirit we have subdued to make them dependent on us. And yet, as G. K. Chesterton wrote in his moving poem, 'The Donkey', 'Fools! For I also had my hour; One far fierce hour and sweet.' A reference to Jesus choosing a donkey to ride into Jerusalem and his crucifixion.

I walk around the empty cathedral with a warm glow, there is a sense of good-natured humour here and a vitality that keeps me from moving on. St Domingo died in 1109, but his power to astonish continued through the fourteenth century. Another painting shows a group of townspeople kneeling beside his coffin, their hands are thrown back in horror, one woman in particular looks as though she is going to faint. The reason is the sight of two white, disembodied hands hovering around the outside of his tomb. In the background the hostile army of King Peter can be seen advancing on the town, which he intends to conquer. The story goes that when the residents of Santo Domingo saw the army, they went to the cathedral to ask for protection. Suddenly, a gentle, penetrating and calming holy wind came out of St Domingo's tomb and blew around the gathered crowd. It was accompanied by two disembodied, snowy white hands which hovered about them. At that moment, the king and his army were struck blind. Realising the error of his ways, King Peter asked the saint for forgiveness and the town was spared. This time, the miracle is a political act as well as a compassionate one, but it is still very amusing.

The *Codex Calixtinus* tells us of many miracles attributed to a range of saints associated with the Camino, right across its extended route from Paris, through France and across Spain to Santiago de Compostela.

> *For a sick man puts on his tunic, and is healed. Through his endless virtue, a man bitten by a snake is healed; another possessed by a demon is liberated; a storm at sea ceases; the daughter of Theocrite is restored after a long illness; a man sick in his entire body is restored to longed-for wellness; a deer, previously indominitible, is tamed to serve him; an order of monks grows with him as abbot protector; a possessed man is liberated from his demons; a sin of Charlemagne, revealed to him by an angel, is forgiven; a dead man is restored to life, and a violated man to his former health; and more, two cypress wood offerings of the bishops carved with images of the apostles arrive from Rome to a port on the Rhone, through the waves and the seas, without anyone steering but solely by his mighty power.*

Inexplicable happenings, strange goings on, justice administered from behind the curtain of normality – miracles have a unique, intriguing power, and they are common across all religions.

Europe was zinging with Christian miracles between the fall of Rome and the Reformation, the centuries we call medieval, before science and reason dismissed them as a by-product of the uneducated, unscientific and illiterate mind. It is a superior and arrogant interpretation from a secular age. Why miracles were important for ordinary people is not easy to answer, but they certainly were in ways a post-Enlightenment world cannot truly understand. There is no one single reason for their proliferation during this time, and no one can claim to understand why they were accepted as part of life, but the fact remains they were, and they still appeal and have an impact.

Academic studies of miracles are in-depth and rigorous investigations into that unpredictable encounter between mind and world. The political, religious and social atmosphere of the time is important, as are the lives of those who are said to have performed them. The reliability of the eyewitnesses, and the competence of those who wrote the accounts down are well scrutinised. My personal conclusion chimes with that of several commentators – whatever it was that actually happened was enhanced to reflect a political, religious and social context. Some of those accretions were born out of hopes and fears in times of sickness and war, others to rebel against political oppression, some asserted the authority of the church, or gave moral warnings; there is a long list of motivations for embellishing stories. Over the years, layer upon layer has been added. Whatever the original incident, the account grew like a snowball rolling downhill. Extracting the kernel of fact from the miraculous story is nigh on impossible, but the core is less appealing to me than the messy but rich human weavings layered around it.

My good friend, theologian and professor of Catholic studies, Tina Beattie, summed up the meaning of miraculous stories:

> They are what they are, touching, amusing, intriguing, thought-provoking, creative yearnings of the human heart that have been passed down through the ages. They gave, and still do give, comfort in the messiness of our lives. Some are very funny, others

touching and beautiful. But mostly miracles are encouragements and maybe even entertainments – suggesting a divine sense of humour perhaps – and we should take them as such.

In modern times, no less than any other age, their role is to let us glimpse beyond the rational, the disarray and jumble of the everyday and to glimpse divine, audacious hope. They part the heavy curtain of natural law and allow us to dream of another reality.

Modern miracles abound, and 99 per cent of them are related to medical cures. To become a Catholic saint, it is necessary to show that two miracles can be attributed to the person being considered. Their veracity is determined by the Vatican-appointed Miracle Commission, a panel of theologians and doctors, who are not necessarily Catholic. The Miracle Commission only decides on medical cures, others such as weeping statues and stigmata, are left to local people to investigate and they can believe them if they wish. Miracles in various forms have always been, and still are, part of humanity's psyche, a desire to see divine intervention in our everyday lives; take them or leave them, but don't deride them, most of us have longed for a miracle at some point in our lives

With a head full of marvellous chickens, I leave Santo Domingo de la Calzada early the next morning, and no word of a lie – a cock crows. The sun glints off wet roads, the air smells fresh, and the red track, empty and inviting, stretches into the distance. A day of the peace of rolling farmland lies ahead, miles of track through fields and birdsong. On a wall someone has scrawled, 'Nature is God's Glitter,' and on a day like today, I'm more than happy to walk along its shimmering paths, and even the hens sparkle a little.

CHAPTER SEVEN

War and Peace

The road goes on, stretching ahead, defining the days and providing direction and containment. It is three days to Burgos in the province of Castile y León, the first major cathedral city. The only visible boundary between Navarre and Castile y León is a tall information sign, otherwise the fields continue uninterrupted. The vast stretch of flat, treeless agricultural land called the Meseta is inching closer, I can feel its presence. For now, though, the Camino passes through ancient, beautiful but empty villages, their heart ripped out over the last few decades as labour-intensive agriculture became mechanised and the farm labourers left to find urban jobs.

A population density map of this part of north-central Spain shows fewer than 26 inhabitants per km^2, a third of that for Spain in general. Once bustling, the streets and houses are largely empty, especially so in these days of Covid; nearly all the albergues, cafés and shops are shut too. The past occupants have not entirely disappeared; their spirits live on in the worn-down stone steps that lead up to haylofts, across the thresholds of churches and on the paths to water fountains – ancient presences that linger long after life's graft has ended. Scratches, scuffs, eroded flagstones – they give credibility to the past.

The mass exodus from rural Spain began in the 1950s and 1960s, prompting a regional journalist, Sergio del Molino, to coin a term for these abandoned places: *España vacía*, or 'empty Spain'. The imprints of the long-gone residents are now overlain by the boots and sandals of modern pilgrims who pass through each year, bringing with them the opportunity for different kinds of employment and a new life force. Settlements along the route have transformed from an economy dominated by agriculture to one largely based on tourism.

Linking the villages is a stone-strewn track, which passes through large fields of regimented lines of dead sunflowers that stretch to the horizon. They make for a weird, dystopian scene. Their stems are almost as tall as me, and the huge, disc-like flowerheads, once so brilliantly yellow, are blackened and hang low in defeat, staring at the soil. The yellow petals that once fringed their sun-seeking centres are curled, brown and sharp as daggers. All the plants face in the same direction, as though struck down en masse when the summer sun went down on them for the last time. I decide to walk along a row, and the razor-edged petals scratch my skin. A distant flock of birds that had been feeding on the oily seeds rises in alarm and wheels away, tinkling and tweeting. Far from the track now, and surrounded by dead flowers, I lie down on the bare earth and look upwards into their bowed, lifeless faces, framed by a grey autumnal sky. They could be an alien army, scorched, and rooted to the spot, and they set a sombre mood.

The road continues uphill through pine and oak woodland, which masks the noise from the N-120 close by. On the top of a rise is a rest area with picnic tables and a war memorial; a square-sectioned concrete pillar about four metres high, which sits inside a black metal fence. The top is larger than the base, giving the impression that a huge concrete nail has been hammered into the ground, piercing the earth. There are barely any decorations, just simple information plaques in Spanish, the date 1936 and peace doves, one on each face. It is as stark and uncompromising as a fact; a plain monument to an ugly truth. In the first months of the Spanish Civil War in 1936, 300 men who opposed the nationalist regime of General Franco were executed by firing squad and their bodies dumped in a shallow pit at this spot. A similar atrocity to the grave on the Hill of Forgiveness. The sign reads, 'This humble monument was built by their families so they will never be forgotten.'

The pillar has a rock-solid presence, a physical representation of the reality of searing grief. Pain is writ large into concrete, a substance that won't soften, change shape or diminish. It stands hard-edged and motionless in contrast to the surrounding trees, to the endless stream of humanity passing by, to the weather, to the turning of the earth. It is a fitting representation. Grief is brutal and angular, not rounded and soft; an immovable, permanent fixture in our inner landscape. The initial shock and intensity after someone's death may subside over time, but the heartache, the empty space, the immutability, the never-fulfilled search for their presence – that becomes part of you. It is inserted into your being and it won't be removed.

Death visits in many ways and at any time – in the womb, in childhood, through age, illness, accident, suicide, neglect; it takes the innocent as well as those who carry guilt, the young and the old. It can bring devastation through the cold-bloodied injustice of murder or war, atrocities that rip life from its moorings in the cruellest of ways.

Does the deep, emotional response to death, that which we call grief, vary depending on the cause? Is grief more keenly felt in some cases than others? I cannot answer that, I have never experienced loss through atrocity, for example, and I have never lost a child, I could never comment. But I do understand why the families chose this form of monument – why they wanted it to look like this. It gives an external shape to an internal state that I recognise. It speaks to me. I sit at its feet.

Diary entry: Scott Polar Research Institute, Cambridge, Autumn 2015

An oak tree is growing in a well-tended lawn outside the entrance to the Scott Polar Research Institute, part of the University of Cambridge, dedicated to the understanding of the polar regions of the earth. At the base of the trunk is a plaque set in granite with a quote from a diary written by a young researcher on a glaciological expedition in the Tien Shan mountains in Central Asia. It reads:

> In memory of David James Sexton who lost his life in the Soviet Tien Shan Mountains on 16th August 1989.
>
> This oak tree is to commemorate David and his love of wild places.
>
> He wrote of the area: 'Huge mountains appeared like a wall, all craggy and covered with snow. We are right in among them, flying up the glacier which is so big, all billowy with beautiful white curves …'

I stare at it for a long while, remembering a gentle, generous, tender friend with dark hair, dark eyes, a profound sense of right and wrong, and with the most delightful, whimsical sense of humour. He had a nickname for me, Mary-bean. David was in love with wild landscapes and he approached them with pure humility. People often say of someone who has died that they never said a bad word about anyone. He really didn't. I place some white roses by the plaque and put my hand on the tree. Winter is well advanced and dead leaves blow across the grass and whirl down from the branches overhead. People constantly come and go; a double-decker bus whines as it stops and

starts. Cold wind, wet ground, overpowering grief. The
last time I stood here was with David's mum and dad and
a scientist from Russia; it was cold then, too. With
nowhere to put the chaos, I leave and walk quickly down
Lensfield Road. This is the only visit I have made since
1989, I haven't been back since.

Rewind to the summer of 1989.

Bristol was warm and wet. It is often warm and often
wet. David and I were standing beneath a streetlight in
the St Pauls area; it was late and dark and rain fell
steadily. We had recently split up – I was too engrossed
with myself and couldn't commit. David was about to
leave for a dream trip, a Russian expedition to collect
samples from glaciers in remote mountains. It was a
sideline to his PhD on the evidence for climate change
in ice cores.

'When I come back, will you marry me?'

'No, it's not like that anymore, I'm so sorry, David.'

He cried, kissed my cheek and walked away.

After he left, I sent him a long letter and a book of
Russian short stories – he loved Russian literature. I
hoped he would like reading them out there in the evenings and that the letter would explain a little more. I
offered to meet up when he returned, and wished him
the trip of a lifetime. I told him what I should have said
under the streetlight. He had left a forwarding address; as
he was gone until the autumn, there was time for them to
reach him.

A few weeks later, I was filming for a documentary in
an opencast coal mine in South Wales. A jeep sped down
the track and a man ran over to tell me there was an
urgent call for me in the office. He drove as fast as he
could. It was David's father. 'Mary, David is dead. I just
wanted to hear your voice.' I held the receiver, unable to

put it down, unable to speak. Everything disappeared. The jeep driver held me. I can't remember his name.

On the last day of the long, difficult and dangerous expedition, the Russian leader needed to make one last climb to collect equipment from the top of a glacier. Only David offered to help, of course he would. They set out early in the morning and climbed the river of ice. By the time they made their way back down the sun had softened an ice bridge over a large crevasse. As they crossed, David in the rear, it collapsed. David dug his axe into the snow in a desperate attempt to stop the slide into the void. The rope that linked him to the supervisor was too long. He fell over the edge. He was 24.

At the funeral in Cambridge his mother handed me a letter addressed to me that was found in his coat pocket when his body was recovered. It was full of his love and hope, funny stories and drawings of his tent and the mountains. He used a similar phrase as on the memorial, describing the glaciers as, 'all white and billowy, like an ocean'. It said how much he was looking forward to coming home and having toast for breakfast. He joked that after eating so much condensed milk over the last few weeks he was now spherical, I might not recognise him, but could we meet up?

Some time later, the book of short stories and the letter came back to me unopened. They had never reached him.

'The biggest mistake is you think you have time.'

I wasn't expecting to meet David on the Camino 31 years after his death. He was as gentle and fun-loving as ever, singing loudly and always out of tune, wearing one of his signature patchwork jumpers, knitted by his lovely and loving mum. Despite being shy his jumpers were a riot of zany shapes and bright colours – everyone wanted one. A pilgrimage wouldn't have appealed to David, he preferred to wild camp somewhere empty and remote, which we often did in Snowdonia or the Lakes. Today, though, we are together again by a memorial on a well-trod path next to a main road. Another gathering place. Lost in the emotion of the moment I don't notice a German couple arrive at a picnic table who break through with a cheery hello and an offer to share coffee. As we pass pleasantries about the weather, the emptiness of the trail, blister control, Covid news and the need to keep moving, I am aware of David behind me, but he is receding, disappearing. When they leave I go back to the memorial, but he has gone. Only the ghost of his presence and a solid sense of loss remain.

Singer-songwriter David Gray explained to me how the Henry Moore sculpture *Two Piece Reclining Figure No. 5*, installed on Hampstead Heath, helped him think through what loss means. Two solid, rounded forms lie side by side, but with a clear gap, or *Ma* (see Chapter 6), between them.

What we see is a deliberate removal, an omission of a whole section of the conceived form. This violation or spatial surgery creates a massive tension and makes the imagination work more vigorously to make sense of what it sees. It decodes and disrupts our ready perceptions of what we are looking at. I still haven't resolved my feelings towards it and perhaps never will. In archaeology or palaeontology ancient fragments are found and pieced together and there's something of the classic Greek form at the heart of these figures. Perhaps he realised the power of all the missing pieces and found a symbol there. Grief slices out whole sections of our lives and the violence of the twentieth century did so on a vast scale. In some ways we are a patched up and improvised mosaic of shattered pieces, each person contains smoking battlefields that are now greened over.

Burgos is a beautiful city and the cathedral is highlighted as a must-see, one of the most impressive in Spain, but frustratingly it is shut by the time I arrive. In a nearby launderette, as I wait for my washing, I read about the city's most famous son, El Cid. This swashbuckling eleventh-century knight and warlord fought for both Christian and Muslim armies. His exploits were so impressive that he earned the Arabic title *al-sīd*, meaning 'the lord'. His many successful battles expanded the kingdom of Castile, and he switched allegiances with ease. Famously, he fought for Sancho the Strong whose tomb I visited in Roncesvalles. El Cid was a brilliant strategist, a creative leader, a learned man and utterly ruthless, slaughtering and executing wherever he went. If he was on your side, you loved him, if not, it was bad news. In the city centre, a statue of El Cid as a war hero shows him splendid atop his beloved horse Babieca, sword pointing forwards, his cloak is blowing in the wind. 'I call to your grace, O Cid, you who were born for grandeur!' says the anonymous, The Poem of El Cid, the oldest Castilian epic poem in existence.

The Camino is a walk through the history of conflict, ancient and modern. Castles, forts, fortifications, memorials, mass graves – they accompany every step. History is proof that humanity is hard-wired to form sides, to fall out, fight and kill; the evidence is everywhere. So much feuding and death, so much loss feels hard to take, perhaps the memorial has drained me. The rhythmic turning of the tumble dryer and the relaxing effect of a beer takes my mind to healing places, to three small islands with a big message. They tell a story the world needs to hear and that I need to remember. They show there is another way to settle arguments that need not involve combat.

Feuding between Scottish clans is legendary, never more so than between the Stewarts of Ballachulish, the MacDonalds of Glencoe and the Camerons of Callart. Yet together they maintained three islands in the middle of Loch Leven, a small loch that sits below the dramatic entrance to Glencoe. Despite its theatrical setting, Eilean Munde, the largest of the three, is not particularly beautiful. Little more than a rocky outcrop, it has the remains of a seventh-century church and a few trees, but also a joint burial ground. Members of all three clans were laid to rest here, although it is said that each had its own landing area, which they never shared. Next door to Eilean Munde is the smaller, heart-shaped Eilean a' Chomhraidh, the Isle of Discussion, where people who were locked in disagreement were dropped off by boat and left alone, face to face. A focussing of minds was encouraged by the isolation, the lack of an escape route, a finite supply of cheese, oatcakes and whisky and the prospect of a cold night if matters couldn't be resolved. Being away from their local politics with its heightened emotions must have helped too. We are told that across the fifteen centuries this custom was in use, only one murder took place, and conveniently the burial isle was next door. Usually, though, the wind, water and the wild worked their magic and disputes were settled. The reconciled parties were then ferried to a third neighbouring island, Eilean na Bainne, the Isle of Milk, so called because it was used for grazing, but it doubled up as the Isle of Covenant. It was here that the settlement was drawn up and sealed. Only then were the two parties allowed to go home.

I love this story and would like to spend a night on the Isle of Discussion, to sleep in a place that saw the forging of peace, however difficult and protracted it may have been. Three undistinguished islands in the middle of a small loch in the Highlands most likely saved much bloodshed. A wise method in many ways, but wisdom doesn't always survive the passing of time.

Burgos marks the start of the infamous Meseta, a high plateau sitting around 800m above sea level and a section of the Camino that people refer to with either trepidation or love. For 180km there is little more than vast, flat cereal fields, almost no shade and scattered, empty villages. It is searingly hot in the summer and bitterly cold in the winter. Some describe it as holding a unique combination of mysticism and practicality. One guidebook says it has 'changeless, shadeless scenery composed of miles of … well, nothing.' It is the mind section of the trail, a place of empty intensity, disorientating, lacking any obvious reference points. It strips away noise and distraction and reduces you to a single, moving point in a vast landscape. Some skip it entirely and take the bus to León.

The people of the Meseta have been described as sober and ascetic with a touch of visionary madness. By contrast, the Andalusians are said to be exuberant, the Galicians nostalgic, and the Catalans practical and down to earth. In summer, it is common for people to collapse on the side of the roads, overcome with heat exhaustion and dehydration. Some experience strange mental states, a kind of Meseta-mind-games-madness, as befell my Mexican friend Angela on her first trip. Those who succumb tell of hallucinations, of experiencing a disconnect in time and space.

As I stand on the threshold of the Meseta I feel daunted by the days that lie ahead; there is no guarantee of company or conversation to lighten the hours. The first section on the outskirts of Burgos navigates large flyovers and scrappy fields, but a line of trees in the distance indicates a waterway, which is too tempting not to savour; flowing water will be in short supply for a while. Time spent by a river is always restful and thoughtful, even on a slippery bank with a motorway thundering overhead. Rustling trees and rippling water sing a duet that soothes and heals. It is 15 minutes of fortification.

Before long, a giant patchwork of fields stretches away in all directions. Autumn is well advanced and the ground is ploughed and bare. Orange, brown, yellow, grey and black squares stitched together by straight roads form this giant, earthy quilt. At times, depending on the light and time of day, the horizon is lost in the merging of soil and sky. Occasionally, a lone tree stands proud, just the one, left for who knows what reason. Defiant in the face of so much flatness, perhaps it provides a slither of summer shade for man and beast. A single tree piercing the horizon is a potent image.

Millennia ago, forests would once have covered the Iberian Peninsula. Over the centuries trees were removed for agriculture, construction, firewood, ship building and charcoal, or forests were set alight in a scorched-earth policy in the many battles that were waged across the land. Fertile plains such as the Meseta were amongst the first areas to be targeted for cultivation and sheep pasture so that even by the medieval centuries it was denuded of its major woodlands, but smaller patches were left standing as part of the agricultural landscape.

Despite the intense deforestation, medieval pilgrims on the Meseta would still have found trees for rest and shade, and birdsong would have accompanied their walk. The fearsome reputation it has today as a silent, treeless desert is due to modern agricultural policies, not purely history or geography.

The straight, empty roads are hard on the feet and the mind. I'm tired of my own head, my circular thoughts; I'm bored with myself. I miss the company of creatures, winged or otherwise, the singing and scuttling of nature-rich farmland. The only signs of life are distant tractors with clouds of dust swirling in their wake; topsoil blowing in the wind across a silent landscape. I have never been to the Canadian or American prairies, but I imagine they are like this. The silence is the most deafening.

On one long day, after a few hours of walking, a sign points to a rest area off the main track, a picnic spot in the middle of a small plantation of poplars. As I approach the trees, the sound of music grows louder. After days of silence, entering the wood is like walking into the middle of a full-throated choir of birds. My head jangles with a cacophony of starling arias, each outcompeting the next. They are so loud, so exuberant, it is utterly transfixing. The trees are quivering with song. I walk outside and the sound fades quickly, walk back in and the volume is turned up to maximum. I have found a natural music box – open the lid and birdsong bursts forth, close it and the songs are trapped inside. It is a good thing no one else is around, because I can laugh and dance and join in – if they can sing in the silence, so can I. It seems to me that the whole of the bird life of the Meseta is in this one picnic spot. They are hopping along the branches of the poplars, pouring their birdy hearts out, they seem delighted there is somewhere to go and they don't care about an audience.

The Estonian poet, Ivar Ivask, describes birdsong as belonging to everyone, their notes falling from the air and into our souls like 'poetry's snow stars'. A veritable blizzard of snow stars is falling today, softening the straight lines of the Meseta, yet this land sings a dysfunctional love song. I am not sitting in a patch of true forest; this plantation is as man-made and utilitarian as a shed. There is no complexity, none of the organic profusion and diversity found in a natural woodland. All the trees are the same species, age, height and girth. It is a construction built to provide shelter, set in the middle of miles and miles of intensively farmed land. Wildlife has been reduced to those few species that can survive a harsh, minimalist environment. I love sitting in this musical grove, I welcome it, yet I feel profoundly sad. It epitomises the destruction that we have wrought over the landscapes of Europe, the ripping out of nature to create miles of monoculture, with scant attempt to accommodate the needs of wild creatures. Wildlife clings onto patches such as this tiny tuft of trees, and as each human generation goes by, silence becomes normalised.

A Spanish Congress of Ornithology report records that Spain has lost 64.5 million birds over the last 20 years, with farmland birds suffering the most, declining by nearly a quarter. Most of the damage is being caused by the industrialisation of agriculture, the increase in monocultures and the use of pesticides. And here I am, right in the middle of that ongoing disaster. Any nuance has been lost, any defining local characteristics of the Meseta have been stripped away. Sameness has replaced diversity. A numbing, utilitarian land obeys a prescribed, controlled cycle of planting and harvesting that conforms to the rigidity of a business model. We need to provide food, but does it have to be like this? Surely, we have the creativity and the intelligence to feed millions AND allow other life to flourish, it is just a matter of policy and will.

The fate of a lyrical bird of meadow and moor, a ground nesting bird called the curlew, epitomises this transition to intensity and has absorbed much of my attention over recent years. It was once a common breeding bird across northern Europe, but since the 1980s has disappeared from lowland farmed regions at an alarming rate. In 2016, another

500-mile walk took me from the West Coast of Ireland to the East of England. Through curlew eyes the landscapes of Ireland and the United Kingdom (and the same goes for much of Europe) are hostile killing fields. Frequent grass cutting to feed cows destroys their eggs and chicks, as well as other wildlife. The high numbers of predators that thrive in intensive farmland, adaptive, intelligent creatures such as foxes and crows, also take a heavy toll. Over the past 20 years, parts of Europe, such as Southern Ireland, have seen a decline in curlews of over 98 per cent, with a decline of over 50 per cent across the UK. The perfect, lethal storm of habitat loss, predation and intensive agricultural practices is stripping beauty and diversity from the land. If we allow curlews some peace and space, they reward us many times over by filling our spring landscapes with a bittersweet, trilling song and our winter shores with piercing calls of yearning. If we squeeze them out, part of us dies with them, that piece of our being that loves wild beauty and all that comes with it. We don't want this to happen, it is just the way it is playing out. Most species are uneconomic creatures in money-driven landscapes. If they get in the way or if they cost money to retain, they fall foul of the system; not always through malice or lack of caring, more often it is simply the result of balancing the books and making a living. There is scant allowance for creatures that contribute only to our hearts and souls. Most of my life is now devoted to saving curlews. Spread out before me, the harsh lands of the Meseta are a reminder of just how hard that fight continues to be.

Evidence of a time where there was more nature and a greater sense of human community can still be found. Dotted across the fields are natural hills or man-made mounds of earth with doors that lead into small storehouses, dug out from the earth and a door placed on the outside.

It is said that some date back 500 years. The Spanish call them 'bodegas'. A famous collection of bodegas forms a ring around the base of a mound that sits proud of the land like a molehill in the middle of the Meseta, near the village of Moratinos. The mound was made generations ago from spoils dug from the surrounding clay soils, which hardened like concrete when exposed to the air. The bodegas were used to store local wines, cheese and cured meats, produce of the many small farms and vineyards that once flourished here. It is like finding a real life Hobbiton, a homely village for the small, furry-footed creatures described in *The Hobbit* by J. R. R. Tolkien.

Many bodegas have front doors that are brightly coloured and decorated with symbols and pictures. Some have wooden benches set against the outside walls, a place to sit and cogitate as the sun rises or sets over the vast horizon, as did Bilbo Baggins that fateful morning when he passed the time of day with a wizard. Some of them are cosy inside with tables, chairs, paintings on the walls, a small stove, a fireplace with a chimney rising out of the top of the mound and electricity for lighting. Others are minimalist, with only candles, a stool and a crate for a table. These were the original man-sheds, where farmers met to chew the fat, physically and metaphorically, washed down with local wines; they are evidence of a thriving rural community that has long gone. It is late morning when I reach Moratinos and explore its collection of Hobbit holes, willing Bilbo to appear. Perhaps it is Meseta madness, or the sound of the wind across bare soil, but I think I can hear him flapping and fussing as he rushes home to usher me inside for tea and seed cake; that would be nice.

Many bodegas fell out of use in the post-war years as European agricultural subsidies saw vast fields of wheat replace the vineyards and meadows. Most entrances are overgrown and their doors are rotting away. An American-British couple, Rebekah Scott and Patrick O'Gara, bought a farmhouse in Moratinos and a bodega came as part of the deal. In a blog from 2007 about their new life in the Meseta they describe the reality of living along the Camino and providing a service to pilgrims.

> *I would like to make some use of ours, someday – it's very near the Camino path, it's always cool in there, it's cozy and dark and very Spanish. A few little stools and a light source of some kind …A chapel for the pilgrims perhaps, with a nice statue set up on the winepress? A cool resting place on hot days? The downsides are apparent already, the majority related to sanitation. Once they've explored, pilgrims routinely use the bodega doorways as latrines. We could make it something free and nice for the pilgrims. But anything nice left unattended is often wrecked, looted, stolen or otherwise spoiled – even in the sweetness-and-light atmosphere of the Camino de Santiago.*

This couple began opening their doors to poorer pilgrims, those who can't afford the usual hostels. A few weeks before I passed by, they wrote another blog post, 'Kinda Like Old Times.'

> *It's a strange, strange year on the Camino. There's a bus carrying pilgrims past León, which is locked down for a couple of weeks. There are a whole lot fewer pilgrims than before. It is nice. Like old times.*
>
> *We've had a few come here to stay with us. Nowadays, without exception, they are the ones who don't have money to stay with Bruno or at the Hostal. They all are very spiritual. Some of them, apparently, are not very functional adults. Like old times, back when there were hippies all along the Way. Free spirits, broken doves, lost boys.*

The pilgrimage has gone quiet. Santiago 2020 is not an easy path for people with no money, as the only places open these days are privately owned. Most have cranked their prices up as far as the market will bear. The privileged sleep on beds with clean sheets. The poor sleep outdoors.

Yeah, just like the good old days.

'Free spirits, broken doves, lost boys' (and girls, presumably), I'm glad the Camino welcomes everyone, whatever their state of repair. It is no surprise these broken battlers and destitute dreamers head for a long line on a map.

It may seem counter-intuitive, but it has been shown that when we work within constraints, such as being given a set of rules or walking a pre-described route, our brains become focussed and more creative; the opposite is true when faced with total freedom. Boundaries redirect energy away from endless decision-making and towards problem-solving. Unconditional freedom may seem tempting, but it is often a route to aimlessness, confusion and complacency, a floundering in a sea of indecision. Whatever needs our attention, be that a spiritual quest, a broken heart, a life choice, psychological distress, emotional damage, regret, loss, disappointment, a stock-taking of life, an illness – whatever it is – all are best examined with an attentive, focussed brain that is freed from too many external distractions.

Without boundaries, we choose the path of least resistance and put in less effort. We become less critical and analytical, less able to detect nuance and variation. When boundaries are set, creative, innovative thinking thrives. Our brains require something to push against, some friction to create the sparks. The Camino is a narrow, definable line on a map, but it is the doorway to infinite possibilities.

None of this is surprising, evolving as we did in a world that daily presented danger and challenge. Whether finding food, inventing tools, building shelter, finding mates, protecting the group, plotting an attack, negotiating settlements, exploring new territories or coping with the unpredictability of weather and seasons, thinking quickly and creatively with whatever was at hand kept us alive. This ancient ability surfaces today in all our social and political structures. People perform best within limits, as long as they are not too severe.

William Wordsworth pondered the creativity that can emerge from constraint in his allegorical poem 'Nuns Fret Not at Their Convent's Narrow Room'. He compares writing a sonnet, which has a defined number of lines and a prescribed rhythm, to a 'scanty plot of ground', but, he argues, it is fertile ground, not barren. Nuns in their convents or hermits in their sparse dwellings are both constrained, but their thoughts can range to the heavens and back. The end of the poem states:

> In truth the prison, into which we doom
> Ourselves, no prison is: and hence for me,
> In sundry moods, 'twas pastime to be bound
> Within the Sonnet's scanty plot of ground;
> Pleased if some Souls (for such there needs must be)
> Who have felt the weight of too much liberty,
> Should find brief solace there, as I have found.

The set route of the Camino is a constraint. Day-to-day decisions about direction and route are removed allowing the brain the freedom to explore. When added to the benefits produced by walking, which is known to help the thinking process, pilgrimage becomes more than the sum of its parts. The regular rhythm and speed of movement of legs and arms, the pumping of the heart, an increase in blood flowing to the brain – all aid cognitive function and a balancing of energies. Body and mind work together, linking the mind to the feet. Pilgrimage may truly help mend the wings of broken doves and set the lost on the right way home. The Camino is an inner and an outer journey.

To my ears, the names of the Meseta towns strung along the Camino sound redolent with history and mystery – Hornillos del Camino, Hontanas, Castrojeríz, Frómista, Carrión de los Condes, Terradillos de los Templarios, Calzadilla de los Hermanillos, Mansilla las Mulas, they suggest the importance of rural industries and agriculture, as well as their vital role in hosting travellers. Carrión de los Condes, for example, once boasted 13 parishes and 14 pilgrim hostels-come-hospitals, which are now just shadows in the dust. For the most part, much smaller communities now offer a welcome break from the challenges of the Meseta. Unexpected gathering places are dotted around, too; special locations that have developed a meaning of their own, drawing travellers to leave their mark – prayers, tokens, messages, stones, mementos – anything at all that declares they had passed through. These mini places of meaning can be a broken windowsill of an old monastery, a recess in a wall, a well; perhaps they mark an ancient holy space that still carries an aura, even though abandonment is all around. Most of these personal offerings demonstrate someone's love in the form of a poem or prayer. Some express a desire for an event in their lives, others offer encouragement to whoever takes time to read them. I find a pile of small hearts made from felt with the words 'Buen Camino' written on them stacked next to a jam jar for a donation. They are sweet and (pardon the pun) heartfelt little tokens. I take a mauve heart and leave some euros.

The Meseta town of Sahagún marks the Camino's halfway point, a true milestone. It is built on the burial site of two martyrs, Facundus and Primitivus. When they were beheaded in AD 300, it is said that milk and honey poured from their necks. The name Sahagún is a shortened version of San Fagun, an alternative to Facundus. A large Benedictine monastery, San Benito, and subsequently a university, both flourished from the ninth century to make Sahagún one of the most important centres of Christian power and learning in Spain. They now lie in ruins. Wars and political disputes contributed to their demise, but more importantly, they fell into oblivion as pilgrimage declined. It is hard to visualise the glory of their heyday amongst the jumbled remains.

My accommodation is in an old, run-down hotel, which is friendly enough. Delighted to have found a room with a bath, I then spend ages trying to explain in increasingly desperate hand gestures that my bath has no plug. All manner of inventive mimicking of a plug going into a hole only serve to alarm the young male receptionist, who literally quakes with terror as I drag him to my room. His relief is palpable when I point to the bath, and all becomes clear. He finds a plug in a cupboard and escapes downstairs at the speed of light. Lying in warm water after days on the road is one of life's greatest pleasures.

Pilgrim street art is a feature of Sahagún, as are colourful billboards with lines of poetry from Emily Dickinson. That most reclusive of American poets seems to speak to the learned, pilgrim soul of this old Spanish town. But it

is not the art I want to see so much as the Iglesia de la
Peregrina (Church of the Female Pilgrim), which stands
alone on a hill above the ring road around Sahagún. I had
been told about it by Angela, the Mexican woman I had
met earlier, who urged me to go there to receive a blessing
that is given only to women, to protect them and give
them strength on their journey.

I had been looking forward to this recognition of
women on pilgrimage; everything I had seen so far was
very male. The majority of the churches and cathedrals on
the Camino are ornate and highly gilded, as much symbols
of wealth and power as gathering places for prayer. Statues
of medieval pilgrims are common, but they are invariably
a romanticised image of solo men striding forth carrying
a staff and a gourd, their cloaks flapping in the wind.
None are of single women.

It takes me a while to find the church right on the
edge of town. Romanesque, square and comparatively
plain, built with bricks, not blocks of stone, its origins go
back to the thirteenth century when it was a Franciscan
convent, and then later a pilgrim hospital. Over the
centuries, war, ecclesiastical disputes, changing fashions
for pilgrimage and a lack of love caused it to fall into
disrepair, until its restoration was completed in 2011.
Today it is used as a study centre and as a pilgrimage
museum.

The transition from being known as the Church of
St Francis to the Church of the Peregrina took place
when a statue of the Virgin Mary dressed as a pilgrim was
enthroned in the seventeenth century. Something about
the image of a travelling Mary, carrying a staff and a
gourd (albeit in silver, and she wears a large silver crown)
touched the pilgrim soul of Sahagún, and women
pilgrims have found her a source of inspiration and

validation ever since. The original statue has been removed to a museum, but a less shiny one now takes pride of place. This much more modest Madonna is wearing a wide-brimmed sun hat complete with scallop shell, not a crown, and her staff and gourd are wooden; a far more fitting recognition of what is needed to travel a long road.

I am the only visitor on this cold, windy afternoon. The steep path from the ring road provides a rare viewing point across the openness of the Meseta, and the miles of beaten tracks I have walked to get here, forged by the footsteps of pilgrims for 1,000 years. The church holds a calmness, and its peace spills outwards and envelops me as I stand by her austere walls. This lonely church has absorbed so much turmoil for so many centuries, but it is still standing strong. I feel a recognition of my solo journey that, quite unexpectedly, brings tears to my eyes.

Inside is bright and airy. Since it is no longer a working church, the vestiges of past devotion are felt rather than seen. Information boards and mannequins dressed as pilgrims line the corridors and give a history of women on the path to Santiago. Many are playing instruments and dancing, some are performing gymnastics. They look young, agile, fit and fun-loving. The main nave of the church is now a large hall and filled with light. There are no pews, which is a pity as my legs are tired and I long to sit in front of the statue of the holy peregrina and her chubby son perched on her arm. She stands on a plain wooden pedestal above a plain altar and below plain, tall, arched windows. Her ornate dress stands in contrast to the starkness all around.

I would love to see this Madonna take life and walk the old, worn paths of the Camino, her dress swishing through

the dust and her gourd brimming over with water scooped
from the many rivers she would have to cross on her
journey. She would plant her feet where millions of hopes
and dreams have trod before. Women and men holding
their faith to the sky and their feet in the mud, their
devotion drawing them onwards.

One of the information boards recounts a Meseta
legend. It is of an old man on pilgrimage, walking
through the seemingly endless landscape that offers little
shade or water. He often becomes faint from exhaustion,
hunger and thirst. Each day, at his lowest ebb, a young
girl appears who is light of heart and foot. She dances
and sings in front of him, encouraging him onwards
with delightful stories and a promise of refreshment and
rest ahead. After many days, when he finally makes it to
Sahagún, he turns to thank her, but she is gone. During
mass, he recognises her image in the loving, welcoming
face smiling down at him from the statue of the pilgrim
Madonna.

I am deeply touched by this tale and what it says of the
role of women in pilgrimage. It is a story of hope and
encouragement. It puts women in a position of strength,
always pointing to a better future, keeping an exhausted
church on track. Nowhere else did I find reference to
singing, dancing and laughter. Catholic religious imagery
is dominated by either agony or ecstasy, there is little
reference to everyday joy. This is the great blessing of the
Church of the Peregrina on the outskirts of Sahagún:
somewhere to smile and be quietly joyful – and to feel
you have a place.

It seems fitting that I am visiting a sacred site that pays
homage to women pilgrims in the year that Pope Francis
published his encyclical *Fratelli Tutti* – '*On Fraternity and*

Friendship'. Fraternity is a term rooted in maleness, in brotherhood, in the companionship of men. Although its aim is to be inclusive, the title shows how maleness dominates western Christian thinking. This calm building sits on the edge of a faith where the vast majority of the imagery and language is dominated by a masculine interpretation. Statistics tell us that as many women as men walk the Camino each year, maybe more, and if that is so, what a pity that there is only this one, light-filled place to mark the significance of that truth.

Sitting in a restaurant that evening in Sahagún I order a glass of wine and raise a toast to Angela for telling me about the Church of the Peregrina, and to all the women who have journeyed, and still journey, alone. The length or purpose of their travels is irrelevant; it is the intent that matters, the sense of agency and confidence. Solitary women have always been the targets of predatory, violent men, even today, and even if they are simply walking home along a brightly lit street in the middle of a major city in the twenty-first century. Women have a right to walk without fear, and we claim that right. I thank those courageous women from the past who undertook pilgrimages at a time when it was far more dangerous than today.

Women rich and poor, young and old, continue to make their mark in their own way and within their own means, forging paths through a world that is still dominated by men. Change comes incrementally, but small steps can still make headway, slowly but surely. Some women face resistance, ridicule and even mortal danger for proclaiming their freedom and equality, but they carry on anyway because some things are too important to ignore. This pilgrimage, my hopes and my prayers have these courageous women at their heart.

Women are well used to their world being skewed towards men; for most of my childhood and working life I assumed men would be in power most if not all of the time. Margaret Thatcher was an anomaly. After leaving university, a frequent question in job interviews was about my intention to get married and have children. Some careers, though, were simply not available, married or not.

Diary entry: Punta Arenas and the Antarctic Peninsula, 1991

Punta Arenas, a Chilean port in Tierra del Fuego, is a land that Charles Darwin called, 'the uttermost ends of the earth'. It sits at the southern tip of South America, and there is nothing beyond this archipelago of islands, maze of mountains, tidal races and impenetrable forest until the sea freezes over 600 miles to the south. I had been backpacking with a boyfriend through the Torres del Paine National Park and we were recouping there after days camping in the wilderness. Angels don't always appear in white dresses sporting wings, they can wear a tracksuit to deliver their life-changing message. A Canadian woman stopped us in the street and asked if we would like to take a three-week trip to Antarctica for $100 each. She explained that an adventure company was taking supplies to the Antarctic Peninsula and wanted to offset their costs by filling the boat with travellers. Her offer was a message from on high.

Nothing was more enticing to me than a continent of ice populated by creatures created for an epic saga. Gigantic seals with fleshy trunks that roar and sway in ferocious battles on rocky shores. Seabirds with two-metre wingspans which glide over the cold ocean, their white wing tips skirting the waves. Flippered barrels, barely resembling birds, waddle across the land until a penguin's comical form transforms into a missile, able to shoot through and out of the water. And in the depths below the icebergs, the leviathans that carry the unenviable burden of humanity's cruelty and destructiveness; the giant whales' mournful songs slice through our conscience like a sword. Who could not want to be amongst all this magnificence. I had yearned to visit Antarctica for as long as I can remember. Yearning doesn't truly capture it, the German word '*sehnsucht*' is more apt, an inconsolable longing that can be so intense it is painful to experience. C. S. Lewis described *sehnsucht* as a rapier piercing the heart. That is what I felt when I thought of Antarctica.

The frigate was an ageing, ex-service ship with the character of a blustering old Admiral. On board was a ragbag collection of backpackers from all over the world. Most of us were under 35, picked up off the streets at random. A pale young Dane spent all his time hunched in the corner of the bar playing chess against himself. He never once looked outside or invited anyone to join him. I challenged him to a match, which he won in minutes. 'Why are you here?' I asked. 'Why not? Not much else to do.' He turned away and started another game. A good-looking American man with carefully tousled blonde hair and designer outdoor clothes described himself as a teacher. I asked him what he taught – he took my hand and looked searchingly into my eyes, 'I teach people to be students of life.' A young, upper-class English woman wore her hair scraped back in a bun, flat shoes and a tweed two-piece; she was constantly worried. When I asked her how come she was on this trip to the far end of the earth her face twisted with anxiety, 'I'm so silly! My parents would be beside themselves if they knew!' I wanted to comfort her with stories of countryside walks

and recipes for jam. I didn't, but Mr American Teacher
found his pupil and they became an item. An over-loud
Australian, recovering from hepatitis he had picked up
getting a tattoo in Brazil, wore shoes made from old tyres.
He had obviously been very ill and was painfully thin.
His black-rimmed eyes were sunken into his skull. A
bored Irish woman constantly complained about the trip
being a waste of money. A shell-shocked shop assistant
from the Netherlands had found herself bound for Antarctica on her first-ever holiday abroad. There were too
many to list, and most of us were frequently drunk, noisy,
adventurous and, to be honest, a little weird. The only job
we had was to help unload fuel barrels at the destination,
in exchange we were given four meals a day, free booze,
our own cabins, and an inflatable boat for trips ashore.

Once across the stormy Drake Passage the ship hugged
the coastline of the Antarctic Peninsula, stopping occasionally to take the inflatables around islands that were
covered in leopard seals or Adélie penguins. In the sound
where the fuel was to be stored, the ship anchored to the
ice by metal stakes. The tide was high and waves lapped
over the ice edge. The offload had to be done quickly
before the sea level dropped; the captain was concerned
about underwater rocks. As we formed a human chain
and rolled barrels, I looked at the glacier stretching away
to distant mountains. It was only two years since David's
death; it looked more menacing than beautiful. A lone
cross stood on a distant bluff, a memorial to a plane crash.
It was a symbol of God in a land that had no need of
churches.

As the light faded and the tide receded, shouting
brought everyone back to the ship. We were underway as
dinner was served in the communal restaurant. As it was

always warm, everyone had showered and changed into light clothes. The captain and crew ate together, the rest of us were seated at long tables. By now, the sound of the boat scraping and bumping small icebergs was common and caused no alarm, but suddenly, a harsh grinding and then shuddering brought the ship to a halt and it began to list. Plates and cups slid off the tables. The lights went off, emergency lighting came on. The captain and crew were yelling, 'Get warm clothes – get on deck!'

The corridors in the underbelly of the ship were sloping and dark, moving through them felt like a dream – heavy-limbed and slow-motion. Both of us layered on clothes and my hands were shaking. Outside, it was hard to stand on the deck; everyone was crowded together against the railings. Hardly a word was spoken, but there was banging and shouting in the background. I felt as though only our collective silence could hold time still and keep fast the solidity of the moment. If anyone had screamed or cried, everything would have fallen apart.

Dark waves slapped the sides of the boat, a rhythmic, cold beating of freezing water on metal. In contrast, the land was beautiful. The sunset-sky was streaked with gold and red, and it tinged the ice-covered mountains with a blush of pink. Icebergs floated by on a sugar-pink sea, carried on the receding tide to the vast ocean beyond. I wondered if this was how it would all end, in the beautiful, bitter Antarctic waters, close to a land of pink ice. I can't remember how long it took before we were told the ship was stable. I was frozen with fear.

The night was spent in the bar, and a tentative lightness returned. People lay on the floor holding hands or sat in small huddles speaking quietly. A Canadian couple, whose cabin was on the upper deck, right by the exit, told me they thought they would be the first to get to the mustering station. They were amazed to find the Danish chess player already in a lifeboat that was still hanging in its cradle, his hands gripping the sides.

Through the night hours, the story was pieced together. An underwater rock shelf had ripped open part of the hull. Water had flooded some compartments causing the boat to list, but it was now contained and should be repairable. As the tide fell, the boat came to rest on rocks, but the captain was confident it would refloat on rising waters, which it did. As stars glittered over the sea, we sailed very slowly to the British Antarctic Survey base of Rothera.

A rope ladder over the side of the ship was the only way into a pitching inflatable that took everyone to shore and the safety of the base. The scientists who were living and working there, all men, were bemused but hospitable. Huskies were still on site, chained just far enough apart to stop fights. By then, skidoos had replaced dog sleds, but dogs were kept on as companions rather than working animals. Most were curled up in the snow. On a nearby beach, a tarpaulin covered a pile of dead seals which had been shot to use as dog food. The huskies' time in Antarctica was almost over, just three years later they were removed from Antarctic bases for good.

It must have been strange for the scientists to have women walking through their world, especially women that looked like us. In 1991, this vast southern continent was still a men–only club, women scientists were restricted to short summer visits on a very few stations. It was a situation I knew only too well.

Back in 1985, when finishing a geology degree, I had responded to a British Antarctic Survey (BAS) advert in *The Guardian* to work in Antarctica. It was a protest

application as there was no chance of being successful. It
stated only fit, young single men should apply because,
'The work is mainly overseas ... the work requires
staff to share tented accommodation in the field.' I wrote
to ask why that meant women were barred as surely
tents were not difficult to come by, or why not have
women-only teams? I received a stern reply, dated 13th
December 1985:

> The law does not require us to employ women in
> these situations. The success of a small isolated com-
> munity such as we have at our Antarctic stations
> depends entirely on the people manning it and we
> have run a successful and happy organisation in
> Antarctica since 1944. Our international colleagues,
> who have manned their Antarctic stations by mix-
> ing the sexes, have had some very unhappy inci-
> dents. Their legislation does not permit them to
> discriminate. We see no reason to run these risks.

The letter went on to say that the nature of the job might
force people to share tents, which was unacceptable for
both men and women, especially if they were married. It
didn't answer my question about why not supply more
tents or employ all-women crews.

I spent months organising a petition, writing to the
Equal Opportunities Commission and lobbying my MP,
David Knox, to ask that BAS reconsider their position.
By 1986, things had begun to change and the process of
accepting women, albeit in a limited way, had begun.
David Knox forwarded a letter he had received from Bar-
oness Platt of Writtle, an impressive and pioneering aero-
nautical engineer and chair of the Equal Opportunities
Commission. It stated that the decision had been made to
trial women in Antarctica in the summer months. Her

letter, dated 25th June 1986, is something I treasure. The last paragraph reads:

> It appears therefore that the efforts of this Commission and the concerns expressed by individuals, including your constituent Miss Mary Colwell, will result in improved opportunities for women to work in Antarctica.

I was so proud to have been just the smallest part of that shift, but it took until 1997 for women to overwinter in Rothera, six years after my unplanned visit. In 2013, Professor Dame Jane Francis was appointed the first female Director of the British Antarctic Survey.

Looking back on that adventure to the Antarctic Peninsula, I realise I had witnessed momentous change. The memories of the battered old ship, the eccentric fellow-travellers, the male-only scientific base, and the realisation of a dream I had held for so long, to visit Antarctica, all came flooding back 29 years later in the medieval town of Sahagún on the Camino Francés in a church dedicated to women.

CHAPTER EIGHT

The Unravelling Road

A flock of grey and white pigeons lifts off the roof of a village church, one of the last on the Meseta, their wings clattering and flashing bright against a slate sky. They look like prayers rising to the heavens. In that intense light just before rain, the world looks hyperreal, the colour saturation dial turned to max. White walls, glistening pavements, neon yellow markers – all are eye-shieldingly bright. The glint of wet sticks gives away a stork's nest on a high chimney. This strange section of the Camino is coming to an end and the suburbs of León will soon appear. The last days have been dominated by empty albergues, empty cafés, empty roads and vast skies, but strangely, not a feeling of emptiness. The sparser the surroundings the more crowded it felt as mental clamourings turned the deserted tracks into a super-highway of thought. Space and airiness became thickened and congested with their binding threads. They wind around the Camino, twisting and tangling as the miles go by. My head is full of images and memories that come to the fore unbidden, released from the pressure of distraction.

Every day, every moment on a solitary pilgrimage is to be part of a constant series of thought-events with different timelines, from the ephemeral to the eternal, most intensely so on the Meseta. It is too easy to retreat and inhabit a mental world rather than the physical one, making everyday sounds important reminders of normality – a barking dog, a car horn, distant voices, they force the reality of the present. One of these noises is a mobile alert – a group WhatsApp™ message arrives with news from home, and I notice one member hasn't posted for a while. I make a note to call at some point. I need to reach the city and take a day to gather these thoughts and recoup, to catch up, and to let my brain and my body rest. My new boots are holding up well and blisters are being kept at bay, but even so, a day off will be welcome.

In a tobacconist I buy a small scallop shell pin-badge to put on my rucksack. The elderly man who serves me is dressed in a pressed suit and has a quiet, dignified manner. He bows slightly and then waves his hand in a gesture that indicates somewhere far away. 'Santiago?' I smile, and he nods respectfully. A Catholic desk calendar and a small plastic statue of Mary in a white dress and blue veil stand by the till, guarding a collection box for charity. In the background an American punk rock song from 1995 blares from a tinny radio, it is 'Killing in the Name', by the band, Rage Against the Machine. Whilst the shopkeeper and I exchange wordless pleasantries the lyrics, 'Fuck you, I won't do what you tell me!' repeat over and over, with a final flurry of, 'Motherfucker! Uh. Uh. Uh.' It is such an uncomfortable juxtaposition, but he shows no sign of recognising the words.

By the time I reach the centre of León it is evening and fine rain is falling on dark, wet streets. Cars, lights, people, shops, noise – they are a culture shock after the quiet contemplation of the wide, quiet Meseta - a day's break here will reset some dials. The brightly lit, modern albergue is on a main road, it serves cheap meals on Formica tables and a few Spanish and French pilgrims are dotted around, mostly in couples; everyone eats in silence two metres apart. The TV news shows that Trump and Biden are still neck and neck in the race for the presidency. Worryingly, a curfew across Spain is likely to be announced and travel between regions might be banned; I still have a long way to go. Navarre is already in stricter lockdown than Castile y León. Someone says the Camino will soon be closed to new pilgrims. I feel a dark wave building behind me, gathering momentum with each day of bad news; I am only just keeping ahead of it. Back in the United Kingdom, 140 people are dying each day, roughly the same as in Spain, and the trajectory is upwards.

My bedroom is sparse but sufficient. It feels wonderful to lie down and know I am in one place for two nights. 'A rolling stone gathers no moss, and a little moss is a good thing on a man,' said the American nineteenth-century naturalist John Burroughs, who disliked travel, preferring to deepen his relationship to the woods around his log cabin near New York, a home-made haven, which he called Slabsides. If you want to learn something new, he advised, go for the same walk twice. I feel the need to be moss-ed, even if only with the thinnest film of build-up from one day. Burroughs is a writer whose observations of nature make the world sparkle with beauty and intrigue; I would love to have met him.

Footsteps echoing down the concrete corridors, some laughter and then the closing of doors bring the evening to an end. Orange lights move across the ceiling, pushed around by car headlights. Despite Covid, León is bustling and after the silence of the past days, it is comforting to be in the midst of humanity again; I sleep for 10 hours.

León is a fabulous city, and I am especially besotted with the thirteenth-century Santa María de Regla de León (Saint Mary, Queen of León), the glorious gothic cathedral dedicated to the Virgin Mary. It is hard to find the right words to describe walking through a palace of light, designed to represent heaven on earth. It is more like a vast, colourful greenhouse than a cathedral.

Shimmering white, red, blue, green, yellow and orange beams filter through 1,800m² of coloured glass, which make up 125 stained-glass windows, including one of the most beautiful rose windows I have ever seen. The building is deconstructed and stripped to a minimum; it feels as though only the sheer audacity and vision of the architects keep it standing. The colourful light catches the statues, the pews, the ornate carvings in wood, and they illuminate the silver casket containing the remains of León's favourite saint, St Froilán.

Once again, the Camino presents a miraculous tale that is both touching and extraordinary, one that echoes messages from elsewhere, rekindling familiar images. Froilán was a ninth-century local boy renowned for his kindness and holiness, who took himself off to the mountains to meditate and live as a hermit. Legend tells us that one day a wolf spied his donkey and attacked it. The commotion disturbed the saint from his meditation, but instead of chasing it away he gazed at the wolf with a look of such love and forgiveness that it lay down and obeyed him. From then, it always accompanied Froilán, carrying his bags over his back like a beast of burden, and never straying from his side. With strong similarities to the later and more famous tale of St Francis and the wolf in Gubbio, this is another allegorical plea for peace and reconciliation with nature, to lay down our arms and find an alternative to revenge and destruction – even with wolves.

After Froilán's death his body was interred in León, but unlike in Gubbio the wolf's fate is not recorded. As the violence of the wars with invading Moors intensified, his remains were taken to various locations for safe keeping. So revered was this holy man that when peace was restored, one monastery in Zamora refused to give them back and it took the intervention of the Pope to come up with a compromise. Half of Froilán was returned to León, the other half stayed in the monastery. So here he is, the wolf-saint, back again in his homeland, taking his eternal rest in an ornate silver chest in a citadel of light, or at least part of him is. I thank St Froilán for making wolves less fearsome and for breaking the mould of revenge, hate and fear. I wonder what the modern equivalent of this story could be? The world could do with some creative environmental leadership to help us to see things differently, to jolt us out of our view of the planet purely as a source of resources and wealth, and very little else. Perhaps St Francis and St Froilán could come up with a plan and let us flawed mortals down here on earth know what to do, because we need inspiration if we are to survive the twenty-first century. If I could communicate through the ether, I would love to show these two nature-loving saints where we are now, how our relationship with the natural world is working out so many centuries later. I would discuss climate change and the biodiversity crisis with them, highlighting the devastating loss of wildlife and tell them that large carnivores, like their beloved wolves, are amongst the most threatened species on Earth. I would like to hear their views on how we are doing as keepers of our wondrous, living home. I suspect they would weep tears of despair.

I am embarrassed to admit I want to touch Froilán's casket with my shell pin-badge – because just a wisp of a vestige of saintly wisdom would be an encouragement to carry on working in conservation with all its loss, grief, complication and conflict – but I resist. Although I am alone in this vast, light-filled cathedral my twenty-first-century head won't allow me to be medieval, not even for one second, even though no one is around to notice or to care.

Back outside in the streets, the gothic feel of the cathedral is reflected in the striking, nineteenth-century Casa Botines, an outrageously extravagant house-come-warehouse designed for a rich business family by the famous architect, Antoni Gaudí. Built on a corner plot, its pointed spires pierce the sky, and a sense of grandeur is enhanced by lighting both inside and out. Over the entrance a sculpture of St George slaying a dragon venerates the Camino's alter ego, one that worships warlords.

León is an elegant city of style and interesting sculptures. A large metal lion is crawling out of a manhole in the middle of a plaza, and just up the street in the cathedral square, a metal statue of a father and son show the tensions between the generations. The father is gazing at the cathedral, pulling on the child's hand to come with him, but the young boy is looking the other way to the shops, anxious to go in the opposite direction. In the shopping area, a giant human figure reclines in the middle of a busy street, and further on towards the river, the well-photographed statue of a medieval pilgrim sits outside the entrance to the Convento de San Marcos, which dominates the large Plaza San Marcos. The grand building was once a pilgrim hostel, then the headquarters of the Knights of the Order of Santiago (which was formed to guard pilgrims), and is now a luxury hotel. It was made even more famous by the film, *The Way*, where the hapless travellers spend an expensive, drunken night after long days on the road. In this Covid-blighted world the Convento is closed and the Plaza is empty of locals and tourists and so I sit down beside the old pilgrim. He is life-sized and dressed in a medieval tunic and hat. He looks exhausted after crossing the Meseta and is leaning against an ancient cross with his hands clasped on his lap. His head is tilted back and his eyes are closed as though resting or in prayer, and his worn sandals are placed next to his bare feet. He is a touching sight, a reminder of the physical exertion needed to walk the Camino, and the toll it must have taken. Together we face the ornate façade of the Convento, so much opulence set against simple endeavour. Rain is falling steadily, dripping down the old man's face and gathering in the rigid folds of his tunic, and it patters on my raincoat. When it starts to trickle down my neck, I leave him to his peace.

On the way back to the albergue the four men I got to know earlier in the journey are sitting in a burger bar, and it is fun and life-affirming to meet them again. They don't say whether they have made their big decisions yet, but they are enjoying the discernment. As they are moving on after lunch, I return to the albergue's cold but cheap canteen, filled with the smell of shellfish stew. Loneliness feels more real now, an empty ache, but the city has been restorative; I am ready to go again for what feels like the beginning of the end.

The day starts cold and bright, and for a while the sun is always just ahead on the track. Once it climbs higher, though, white clouds race across an azure sky. It is a beautiful walk out of León, through the outskirts and on to the industrial satellite town of La Virgen del Camino, marking the last of the urban sprawl. Now there is a choice to be made between the traditional route, which follows the main road, or a scenic one, which goes through farmland and a sparse scattering of ancient villages; it is more remote but far more enticing. After getting lost trying to navigate a spaghetti of highways, I eventually find the right underpass. On the wall someone has recreated a small section of a prehistoric cave, complete with a hunched bison and handprints; next to

it is the message, 'The whole world is our Altamira Cave.'
Altamira, located on the northern coast near Santander
and only a couple of hours' train ride away, is home to one
of the best examples of prehistoric cave art in the world,
dating back 36,000 years. The exquisite charcoal and ochre
bison, boar, deer and horses, even the human-like creatures,
are drawn with skill and understanding. The artists lived as
hunters and gatherers in an Ice Age world unlike anything
we have in Europe today. No one knows exactly what
they represent, but the figures suggest a deep reverence
and connection to the natural world that has largely been
lost. Decorating the more inaccessible reaches of the cave
system and executed with a true artist's eye for detail and
movement, the cave art shows that our ancestors
comprehended the complex relationship we have to the
rest of life on Earth, a truth that has been so eroded and
distorted as to be unrecognisable today. Graffiti scrawled
on a scruffy underpass on the Camino speaks more about
the true nature of humanity and our relationship to nature
than a thousand wordy environmental-policy documents
and hollow, greenwashed pledges.

The ancient walkway is soaked in thoughtfulness, and
the freshness of the day makes it easier to focus rather
than be led by random, mental meanderings. The space
and light allow for a gathering of ideas from the past days,
and they begin to consolidate into an unfolding story. I
feel much fitter than when I started, a full three weeks
ago. My pack is less tiresome and my feet have adapted to
the constant pounding of hard tracks. I stop at a sheltered
spot and call my husband – it is our wedding anniversary
and although we are spending it in different countries, we
are still very much in the same place as 24 years ago. The
bright air and the red soils make for a vibrant backdrop,
and I use the phone's camera to show him the track

stretching ahead, the trees blowing in the wind and the puddles reflecting the clouds. Setting off again I see no one, no cars, no people – nobody. In solitude you don't need to impress the world, giving it a chance to make an impression on you, and I find I am fascinated by the scenery and the interplay of wind and cloud and horizon.

And then the phone rings.

It feels like a plaster being ripped off skin, exposing and raw. In an instant the security blanket of the Camino is gone. What was known and comforting just seconds ago is now an obstacle to escape from. I have to find a way off this trail, to tear myself from the road and find any transport back to León, then Madrid and then home. Panic and disorientation replace feelgood. In a mile I reach a small village, the bar is the only place open and two men are drinking beer inside. I ask in faltering, panicked Spanish if there is any way to get to León? I expect them to laugh and say of course not, but, amazingly, there is a bus passing close by in two hours, so I drink coffee and wait. My hands are shaking, I keep dropping things, the world is insubstantial and unfocussed. The Camino has completely disappeared, as though it has been absorbed into the landscape. It is irrelevant.

Social media is a depository for pithy sayings. A common one shows a candle glowing in the dark or a shaft of light penetrating woodland with the words, 'Light will always overcome the darkness.' It isn't always true. Sometimes, blackness is a devouring, suffocating, terrible thing. It seeps into a heart and smothers hope, bit by bit. The family member who had gone quiet on WhatsApp™ lost the will to keep on trying to shine and let go. Life held no comfort or light, there was nothing to reach for. Darkness won.

I never made that call, the one I promised myself I would just a short time ago; I didn't get round to it.

'The biggest mistake is you think you have time.'

Back in León my two Mexican friends had jumped on a train to be with me for the evening; they had stayed longer on the Meseta and had only just reached Sahagún. We eat pizza and drink hot chocolate and they hold my hand. It is still dark when they walk with me to the station early the next morning. I remember very little of the flight and the coach home. I have to quarantine and then emerge to face the sheer pain of lives torn apart, of assimilating and comprehending a new world.

We cry and hug. We go to the local park and hold the fronds of a cypress tree whose branches hang low. Its scent is rich and comforting and perfumes the wintry air. Cypress oil has been a symbol of spirituality and immortality since antiquity, and its green, earthy spiciness is used in masculine fragrances. On windy evenings the branches tug and sway as we hold them, as though the tree is communicating; we imagine it is a message to tell us it is OK, now there is peace. In the evening we stand outside and look at the stars, maybe there is a new one up there, a faint light that is finding its feet in the heavens, shining ever more brightly as it settles in its place. In the eastern sky the Planet Venus glows in the darkness, a sentinel of hope.

There are so many practical arrangements to make, so much to sort out, so much time spent waiting for paperwork. The air is thick with shock, grief, disbelief, anger, pain, fear … the days filled with a raging, broiling sea of emotions.

And then there is the hell of a Covid funeral, a sparse, distanced gathering for someone who felt isolated in life and now in death. This is so wrong. People watching online rather than standing together in pews, a few family members spread out in a church, unnaturally distanced. Months later, as news emerged of 10 Downing Street parties when social gatherings were banned, anger reached boiling point. A Conservative MP for Newcastle-under-Lyme in Staffordshire almost broke down in Parliament when he described the day his family buried a much-loved grandmother. 'I drove for three hours from Staffordshire to Kent … I didn't hug my siblings, didn't hug my parents … does the Prime Minister think I am a fool?' His distress is evident on his face. The answer is simple. Yes, Mr Bell, it seems Boris Johnson took all of us for sheep-brained idiots, and he raised a glass to our folly.

After a disorientating month, at the end of November, I must decide if I am to return to Spain and finish the Camino or wait until spring. If I go back now, it will be colder and wetter, perhaps with snow on high ground, more places will be shut and there will be few, if any, people on the trail. There is the added complication of rising Covid cases and another lockdown is increasingly likely. If I wait for next spring, the weather will be better and the days longer and brighter. Perhaps there will be more hope in the air and there will be flowers instead of bare soil, more birds will be singing and the cycle of life will hold eternal lessons. Wait, said everyone, just wait, it's too late in the year, too risky, too everything to go back, and so close to a tragedy.

It is obvious what to do.

Gatwick is eerie. Empty corridors stretch away with no one rushing or pushing trollies. The departure board shows only a handful of destinations, the last one at 17.00

is mine to Madrid. Travel feels different to how it was at the end of September, it is more serious, quieter, stricter. Cautious concern permeates the air. A mask, a recent PCR test and strict distancing are mandatory.

The whole world has shifted since I have been in the United Kingdom. In dramatic elections, the Donald Trump era is over and Joe Biden is waiting to take his place in the Oval Office, but the transition is fraught and tense as Trump refuses to concede. The number of confirmed Covid cases passed 60 million worldwide, although there is more hopeful talk of a vaccine. Newspapers are reporting that November 2020 is the warmest ever recorded.

As a distraction, I listen to a BBC Radio 4 series, a dramatic version of the book *Grief is the Thing with Feathers*, by Max Porter. It is a powerful and original work on loss, love and the poetry of Ted Hughes, and I came across it at exactly the right time. It tells the story of a dad and two little boys who suddenly lose the rock in their lives, their wife and mother, to an accident at home. Told with a fierce quirkiness laced with compassion and humour, at times the book takes the perspective of the dad, then the boys and then Crow. The black-feathered trickster and antagonist is an odd visitor at a time of despair, but he moves in anyway, becoming a heart-healer and part-time babysitter.

Crow is death personified, an unsentimental, sorrow-eating, gall-dripping, cackling, unwelcome guest. Crow reminds the family of his image by leaving black feathers around the house, plucked from his hood. Crow usually has no time for humans, he says they are only interesting to him in the midst of grief, and this family is the embodiment of grief. Motherless children, says Crow, are pure crow, and he cannot help but take advantage and raid this nest, of 'ripe, rich and delicious sorrow'. Crow is a natural cross between a scavenger and a philosopher, and he has a purpose to fulfil. Crow is not there to see the family through their journey of grief, but to navigate the deadening sense of hopelessness. At first, the dad, a Ted Hughes scholar, can only see an empty future filled with well-meaning visitors who don't know what to say. Not so, says Crow, grief is personal and never truly disappears, but hopelessness does, and he is right. Eventually, as days turn to weeks which turn into months, the intense grief that has permeated every waking moment gives way to gentler memories and the family begins to heal. Crow leaves.

León seems quieter than before, there are fewer people on the streets and noticeably fewer cars on the roads. I head straight for the cathedral. Maintenance work in a side chapel intrudes into the dignified atmosphere, drilling, banging, talking. It is only when I close my eyes does the Gregorian chant playing softly in the background break through. It takes a moment of stillness for the ethereal to rise, and I want to sink into the music as though it were a soft bed floating in the air. I want it to carry me for a while, to take my heart somewhere far away, suspended and timeless above this discordant world.

A last walk around brings delight in the form of a thirteenth-century stone carving of a pregnant Mary. She is similar in demeanour to the smiling, rosy-cheeked statue found in the cave at Santa Maria la Real, only this Mary is standing, not sitting. A young, sweet-faced Madonna looks into the distance with one hand resting on her swollen belly. I am drawn to her enquiring, open face that seems to be asking so many questions of the future. The statue is called Our Lady of Hope and she forms the centrepiece of the Chapel of Hope, names that are now laden with significance. I light a candle and leave to rejoin the track to Santiago.

As quickly as they had disappeared a month ago, the yellow way-markers materialise once more; the Camino is reforming, hardening up, becoming an entity again. Just a few weeks ago it had vanished beneath my feet as the storm broke, now it stretches ahead, a solid 1,000-year-old certainty, and I step back on.

A wrong turn on the outskirts of León plonks me in the middle of major roadworks with trenches, jackhammers, tarmac, workmen in high-vis jackets and a man in a large machine. I'm self-conscious and embarrassed, knowing I shouldn't be there; my presence has stopped work and all eyes are on me. As I get close to the machine, the driver leans forward in his cab to speak to me. Only then do I realise he is the spitting image of James Rebanks, the Cumbrian sheep farmer and award-winning writer. The resemblance is so startling I expect him to start telling me about Herdwick sheep, but instead he points towards the Camino with a look of kind forbearance. The workmen stand back as I pass by, watching me step over the cables and piles of rubble. I feel like an idiot as I keep saying thank you, and they nod politely.

The town of La Virgen del Camino is my first overnight back on the trail. One modern hostel is still open in a new development on the outskirts of the town; all the new builds are square, concrete and hard, a counterpoint to its ancient roots. A small supermarket supplies some picnic things for dinner and then I walk along the deserted main street. The impressive modern basilica, said to be the most notable piece of modern architecture on the Camino, is Brutalist in style and built on the site where Mary is said to have appeared to a shepherd in 1505. Dominating the exterior is a remarkable façade from the late 1950s, a frieze of thirteen, six-metre bronze figures representing Mary and the twelve apostles. They tower above, and each one is holding a symbol of their life or death. St Matthew holds out a stone, representing his martyrdom by being stoned to death, and his neck is cut to show his beheading; St Bartholomew was skinned alive and carries a knife; St Simon is leaning against a saw, the instrument of his torture and death; and St James is pointing towards Santiago and is covered in scallop shells.

Inside, it is cool, sparse and meditative, but a feeling of agitation keeps peace at a distance. Across the street is a large Dominican convent, I immediately recognise the Order's black and white symbol and the motto 'Veritas' (Truth) written beneath. That same symbol was on a metal badge that was pinned to my school beret, the uniform of St Dominic's Convent School in Stoke-on-Trent. It is strangely comforting to see it here. The sound of trickling water turns out to be a small pool, fountain and grassy area in the middle of the car park, and as the gates are open and there is no sign to say keep out, I go in. The pool is just a decorative feature, Zen-like and calming. Different-sized boulders have been carefully arranged in the pool to give points of solidity and strength, an unyielding presence amidst the slow flow of water. The branches of willows brush the surface in a soft caress. It is so soothing that I sink onto the grass and watch autumn leaves drift and bob on the ripples. It is the first time I have let go in a month and a wave of peace washes over a fractured inner landscape. I think about the friendship between St Dominic and St Francis and their dedication to helping the poor, and about the Dominican love of learning. Dominican philosophy is rooted in the search for divine truth, through finding it in everything, everywhere. By study and good works, said Dominic, it is possible to glimpse the heart of God – truth itself. I ponder on the famous story about St Dominic, who sold his expensive books inscribed onto sheepskin parchment and gave the money to the poor: 'I could not bear to prize dead skins when living skins were starving and in need.'

'Can I help you?' A man has appeared on the tarmac. I tell him I am just looking at the water for a while and I hope that is OK. 'You must leave,' he says, 'this is private ground.'

The next morning the hostel owner offers me coffee and asks me to let her know when I get over the high passes that lie between here and Santiago. She tells me she's concerned that I am alone, especially given that snow is forecast. Her kind words and concerned eyes make me cry.

Within minutes, I am back in the underpass with its cave-art graffiti and head to the more remote route, the same red, stony track that leads through ploughed fields; it looks just as it did a few weeks ago. This late-November day brings a gentle breeze and the soft tweeting of birds, I am grateful, a cold silence might have been unbearable. I have no choice but to walk the same way, past the spot where I received the call, and I walk straight on. The road that became so insubstantial is now welcoming and pulling me forwards. I go directly through the village where I caught the bus back to León, veering around the bar. With every step, the invisible area of turbulence is left further behind. This is new territory, breathing becomes easier. I am on the other side.

CHAPTER NINE

Stones and Snow

I have extra weight to carry in my rucksack; the top pocket is now filled with a bag of memories – stones, jewellery, fronds from a spruce tree, shells, various small mementos, private messages written on tightly folded pieces of paper, even milk teeth. The last few days in England were spent collecting whatever people wanted me to place on the large mound of stones that form the base of a towering icon of the Camino – the Cruz de Ferro. Three must-see places are marked on the map across northern Spain – the first is ticked off, the sculpture on the top of the Hill of Forgiveness, the second is the Cruz de Ferro, the third is the cathedral at Santiago.

The Cruz de Ferro, the Iron Cross, is a few days walking away yet, but I can feel it getting closer. It stands at the summit of Mount Irago at 1,504m above sea level and holds a special significance for many people, described as a powerful place to perform a ritual, and as a shrine for contemplation and spiritual release. It takes the form of a huge pile of stones, which surrounds the base of a five-metre-long wooden pole topped with an iron cross. Mounds of stones in the form of cairns have been used for thousands of years to mark pathways, sacred places or the tops of mountains, and this may have been the pre-Christian origin of the stones around the Cruz. In the twelfth century the hermit monk Guacelmo is said to have used an ancient cairn to support a pole and cross, perhaps as a visual guide for pilgrims or to claim the site for Christianity. This is one explanation, but many stories claim its origin, and which one you pick doesn't really matter. It is there, towering above a beautiful vista and it has the reputation for being profoundly moving. Tradition has it that before you walk by you add your own stone or memento, leaving it behind to represent a burden offloaded or an offering. Over the years, millions of tokens have been piled high on this mountain, and in just a few days, my bag of memories will join them.

The flatness of the Meseta has been replaced by rolling farmland as the trail heads for the next ridge of high ground. The landscapes and villages are lovely but deathly quiet; in the month I have been away the feeling of shutting-up and closing-in has intensified. Brewing tea on a camping stove by the side of empty stretches of road feels dystopian; I could be the only person on Earth. The increased sense of isolation brings to the fore more questions, particularly on the history of the Camino and what is says about the rise of Christianity in the West. Wars and violence sit alongside the Christian stories of redemption and love; it plays with your head. Other religions were either subdued or eradicated as it took control, often ruthlessly. What legacy has it left after 2,000 years, both spiritually and psychologically? They are questions faced head-on by Graham Greene, whose novels I have been re-reading throughout 2020.

The 2002 film of Greene's *The Quiet American* fills a solitary evening in an empty albergue – even the owner has left the site. I watch it on my phone, lying on a dormitory bed. It is set in 1950s Vietnam, a tale of tangled love played out amidst the breakdown of French colonialism and the beginnings of the American involvement in the Vietnam War. As with all his work, flawed characters spin a complex story and produce a thought-provoking book. Cultural dominance, the ethics of war, personal morality, the succour and dogma of religion – particularly Catholicism – are heartland topics for Greene, and he plays them like the strings of a violin.

The eternal questions Greene lays bare are the same as those faced by any one of us who feels wholly unfit for the challenge of living truthfully in a world that continuously confronts belief and conviction. My words can't better those of blogger and literary critic, James Mustich:

> In his best novels, Greene's talents combine to transform page-turning into a kind of pilgrimage, amplifying the what-happens-next of the narrative at hand with the more mysterious what-happens-next in which our lives unfold. The distinguishing landmarks of the alluring literary landscape known as 'Greeneland' are the questions of virtue and desire, rectitude and compromise, shame and salvation that we'd ask ourselves if we had the time and courage to ponder the meaning of our own motives and activities. Engaging us as readers first and as seekers second but more lastingly, his novels remind us of something we already suspect but seldom articulate – a conviction that life must have higher stakes than we are wont to play it for. What gives his work its enduring hold on our imaginations is his uncanny ability to capture between covers the suspense in which our souls exist. Really.

Greene travelled widely but never undertook a pilgrimage as such; his was a quest addressed through fiction informed by travel, but it amounted to the same thing. The opening words of the second volume of his autobiography read, 'What a long road it has been.' He faced real dangers as he witnessed profound social and political changes. Few can match his skill to put into fiction the pain and the glory of life, the questioning of right and wrong and the many shades of grey in between. Through tortured lives he exposes the raw power of religion to dispense redemption or damnation; he exposes how lives are fated by faith, politics and social expectations. The Camino has seen all this and more, many times over. It has held numerous individual torments and it has experienced the violent transition of political power, the painful clash of cultures which is now evident in the statues, the stained glass, the tombs and the paintings. In a silent albergue on a cold, clear night at the end of November, Greene's uncomfortable questioning of what is morally right and who defines it rise to the surface, questions I had asked myself years before but had never found a resolution. Now, with time and a unique environment for contemplation, they inhabit the night hours. What is the relationship between culture and religion, which has precedence, and who decides? The Camino gathers memories like stones on a cairn.

Diary entry: Eastern Highlands Province, Papua New Guinea, 1993

The small plane spiralled down through a hole in the clouds to land on a grassy strip on top of a mountain. We had been circling for a while, waiting for a gap to appear, and suddenly the plane dived. Never had I been so glad to be on solid ground. Metal cases of camera equipment and supplies were unloaded as small, wiry Sambia people put them into string bags and hung them over their foreheads, the cases resting against their backs; I was sure their necks would snap. As the plane took off and the sound of the engine faded, I felt disconcerted as well as excited.

The village was a day's walk through upland farms, steep mountain trails and over ravines. Logs bridged smaller streams, but wider, deeper gorges had rope bridges. Waiting for my turn to cross a particularly insubstantial one, I looked into the gorge – it seemed a long way to fall into fast-flowing water strewn with rocks.

After a few hours, an old man broke away from the group and handed me a piece of sugar cane, which he had cut from a field. It was a kind gesture, but I noticed he avoided eye contact, the only connection was with a nod of his head.

We were given rooms in thatched huts. Inside was dark and smelled of charcoal and woodsmoke, outside was wet and verdant. We were there at the request of the Sambia to film the last initiation rites to be performed on young boys to prepare them for warriorhood. American Seventh Day Adventists, a Christian sect, had arrived in the village and the old ways were disappearing under a cloud of shame and reorientation. Churches and a Christian God were replacing traditional beliefs, which the missionaries considered sinful. Over the next few days, warrior rituals and a traditional marriage ceremony would be carried out for the last time, and they wanted it to be recorded in a documentary.

Any interpretation of another culture is swayed by what is viewed as normal for the observer, it is a reality that field anthropology tackles every day. Every human society is multifaceted, can any outsider truly grasp the complexities? Highlighting one aspect because it is unfamiliar is understandable, but it can lead to disproportionate stress being placed on it, resulting in a distorted picture of the culture as a whole. I don't know if that is the case below, but it is worth bearing in mind. Everything I understand about the Sambia comes from the work of American anthropologist Gilbert Herdt, a specialist in human sexuality, who lived with and studied their culture for many years.

For generations, different mountain communities in the Eastern Highlands Province fought each other for honour, land and women; there was often distrust and antagonism between secluded villages. Life was shaped by cycles of attack and revenge; safety could only be guaranteed by training boys to become fighters. How they did this was revealed to the outside world by Gilbert Herdt, now a professor at the California Institute of Integral Studies. As far as

I know, the following practices have stopped, but the memory lives on in those who took part in them and in the books and films that have been written about their lives. The BBC documentary we made was called *The Guardians of the Flutes*; I was a field assistant, the producer was Paul Reddish and Gilbert Herdt accompanied us on the trip.

Semen played an important role in traditional Sambia warrior culture, it formed the essence of maleness; semen gave a man the strength and courage to protect the village. To lose it was to be made weak and effeminate. Much of what happened to men, boys, girls and women was founded in these beliefs.

When small, boys stayed with their mother in the home. From around the age of seven, they were removed and taken to live with men and adolescent boys in a dedicated men's hut. They would not spend time with women again until they married.

The first phase of initiation was to toughen the boys through sleep and food deprivation and by beatings with sticks and stinging nettles, plants that had a far more painful sting than nettles in the UK. As they were young, they did not produce their own semen and they were made to drink the semen of the adolescents to build their strength. In turn, teenagers replenished theirs through oral sex with older men, and, in turn, the men went into the forest to drink the white sap from particular trees. The older men also played ritual music by blowing on special flutes, which represented penises. All of this was carefully controlled and subject to strict laws.

Sambian men were taught that sex with women took away a man's strength, and that menstrual blood was polluting and dangerous; to touch or even smell it could result in illness and death. For this reason, a woman's genitals had to be lower to the ground than a man's, and a woman entering a hut with men inside had to shuffle on her knees. There were different paths through the village for men and women.

Marriage was always arranged and children were conceived only within marriage. It was believed that to produce a baby, semen had to mix with the internal blood and fluids of women, which was only possible when she menstruated. As nutrition was poor, and girls did not start their periods until aged 18 or 19, young couples were only allowed to have oral sex until she started to bleed. After menstruation, penetrative sex was allowed, but only in the forest and away from society. When menstruating, women lived in a hut separated from the village. Even the smell of women could weaken men, and many put aromatic herbs in their noses before sex. After the birth of a child, a man was not allowed to have sex with his wife for two years, so some took two wives to alternate the arrival of children.

Women had their own rituals which men were not allowed to see, and so less is known about them. It was both a privilege and disturbing to be invited to observe the Sambian women preparing young girls for marriage. As the male film crew captured the boys' initiation, a line of teenagers was brought into a clearing with their heads bowed and covered. They sat in a circle, facing inwards. The older women walked around the outside hitting them on their backs with sticks, though it looked more ritual than forceful. The singing and chanting reminded them that from now on the happiness of childhood was over and a life of toil, physical work and childbearing had begun.

It was a shocking world to enter. To a western mind it was ruthless and cruel, and yet the people were not brutal in their everyday lives, the Sambia were kind and thoughtful. The women were intrigued by my dress and lifestyle. They were funny, too, joking with me and each other; there was a warm female companionship which many westerners would envy. As they worked in the fields they chatted and laughed together, then ate yams around a fire. When they saw me try to wobble over log bridges, they ran over to hold my hands, walking backwards until I reached the other side, then clapped and cheered. They invited me to the fireside to sit with them as they made grass skirts. When I wanted to bathe, they took me to a secluded part of the river where they knew I could be alone.

My life could not have been more different to theirs. Looking into the eyes of the older women, there was a gulf between us, but I could detect no desire to be like me, to have what I owned or to wear the same clothes. Theirs was a fierce and independent spirit. It was the younger women who wanted to leave the mountains for the city, to wear western clothes, to choose their husbands and to have jobs and all that comes alongside it. The men were polite and respectful, but we had little direct contact.

Sambian traditions brought stability to a harsh and dangerous world. The older generation saw the rites as necessary to keep them safe; the men and boys had a defined social structure and a release from sexual tension that kept them focussed on warriorhood. The women supported that role. The world of the Sambia, though, was changing, the younger generation no longer wanted their lives to be governed by a fear of war. They were being taught different ethics in a school built by the Seventh Day missionaries. The men's hut had been converted to a church, and the special flutes that were once used in male rituals now called people to Christian services, much as bells do in the West. New buildings were square, not round, and they were not divided in two, as was traditional. In the past, men and women lived in separate areas of a hut, men at the back, women at the front, but increasingly, husbands and wives lived and slept together.

The American missionaries entered the Sambian world with an attitude of cultural dominance. They lived away from the village in a large, American-style house with a defined boundary fence, which the locals were not allowed to cross. We were invited to visit them, and we could have been in any suburb in North America. Large photographs of members of their family graduating from bible school hung on the walls, they had armchairs and a western-style kitchen. Being sent by God to save the souls of sinful warriors didn't mean fitting in. Seventh Day Adventists do not permit tobacco, caffeine or alcohol and they do not allow any form of homosexual activity.

The Sambia were on the brink of a new world view. They accepted the missionaries and their message, and they appreciated the medicines, the education and the more nutritious foods they brought with them. Children were healthier and far fewer women were dying in child-birth. The elders were taught to value the mountains and had been advised against selling their land to a logging company. And yet, problems were arising the village had rarely seen before, such as rape, theft and pregnancy out-side of marriage. And the root of all evil, money, became a new reason for war.

Towards the end of the trip, two young men arrived from a neighbouring village to demand money from the rich westerners. They told the chief that if thousands of dollars were not paid by nightfall, they would launch an attack. The villagers prepared for war. The tusks through the men's noses, normally worn pointing downwards, were turned upwards as a sign of aggression, and they carried bows and arrows. Women and children retreated into their houses. That night a delegation was sent to explain no money had been, or would be, exchanged. This visit was by invitation, it was not a financial deal. We spent the night sitting in the chief's hut and we were not allowed outside. Our presence had triggered a new reason for aggression – money – a sign of changing times, new values and a different set of tensions.

As the old ways were shamed out of existence, so was the role of sex in society. Just before we arrived, a six-year-old girl was raped by a teenager. An old man told us, 'No one knows the rules anymore, there is no structure, no release, now anything can happen, and we can do nothing about it.'

When the documentary was completed, it was sent to the elders for approval, only then was it screened as part of the BBC anthropology series *Under the Sun* in 1994.

The questions posed by the Sambia's traditional way of life continue to haunt me 30 years later. I intensely disliked the arrogance of the missionaries, their assumed cultural and religious superiority and the shame they imposed on the local people. So much uniqueness was lost as a uniformity spread through the mountains. On the other hand, the rituals and the basis of relationships were abhorrent to a western mindset – they challenged me to my core – as did an existence based around the constant fear of violence and war. The Sambia join me in a deserted albergue in northern Spain on a cold winter's night, a strange place to remember them.

I wonder what it is like now in those cloud-covered mountains in Papua New Guinea. Many of the older people will have died, embattled warriors with no more wars to fight. Are the new generation living differently? Are they still blowing on the traditional men's flutes to call people to worship? Does anyone talk about the old ways anymore? I know I will never go back to see how things have turned out, but I can tell their story as I saw it many years ago, and I can leave a stone for them on an ancient cairn.

The road between León and the Cruz de Ferro is littered with delights. The extraordinary town of Hospital de Órbigo has a breathtaking medieval bridge supported by 20 arches spanning 200m. It is a complete overkill for the modest flow of water that now runs beneath just a couple of them, but pre-1951, before a dam was constructed upstream, it crossed over a much more substantial river. The large meadows around the bridge were the site of many battles, including a famous year of jousting in the fifteenth century, where one gallant knight broke over 300 lances in a failed attempt to impress a lover. I eat alone in a restaurant where all the tables and chairs are stacked to the side and out of use. There are no other visitors here and the albergue dormitory and the road outside are eerily silent. Frost forms overnight and the stars shine very brightly. I leave early along dark, deserted streets, the only food available is from a vending machine.

By late morning the utterly whacky House of the Gods comes at just the right time for a break. It sits on top of the hill above the city of Astorga, a rest station, hippy hang-out, self-serve café, and chill-out station in the middle of a plantation of trees. As usual there is no one around, not even the owner, and so I spend half an hour looking at the various Buddhas, indigenous face masks, digeridoos, Hindu wall hangings, pagan characters, Buddhist prayer flags, Jewish symbols, Islamic signs, Christian crosses, crazy paintings, and I try out the various hammocks and bean bags. Teas, coffee, fruit and biscuits are left out with an honesty box, as well as produce from the vegetable garden. When the owner does arrive, all smiles and welcome, we exchange small tokens. This place is a joy, and it is very modern Camino.

Astorga's old, creaky, atmospheric albergue is at the top of the town and I make tea and eat most of a box of mantecadas (the town's speciality cakes) on the floor of the dormitory. The large murals that decorate many of the town's buildings showcase historic battles but also celebrate local industries and rural produce, including the town's famous chocolate. Astorga has always been a meeting point for ancient routes through Spain from as far back to the Romans and beyond. It is used to visitors of all kinds, tourists as well as pilgrims, and despite Covid it has an open, welcoming feel. In the evening people safely gather in the main square to drink hot chocolate from a kiosk while their children run around. More of Gaudí's stunning architecture is on display, shining in the dark, dominating and fanciful. At dawn the view out of the dormitory window is spectacular. A multi-layered sky of orange, grey and red illuminates the land I have walked through over the last few days, and somewhere in the middle is the line of the Camino, a path in the dust that has supported me through dark days, and I am deeply and profoundly glad it has brought me this far.

I am now only a couple of days from the Cruz de Ferro, and the closer I get the heavier my bag of memories feels; it's as though they want to be offloaded.

Dawn is breaking as I reach it after a steep walk along a trail that shadows the LE-142. This isn't a secretive place; it is right by the side of a main road. There is a chapel in the trees and two large car parks with picnic tables. A lorry is idling in one of them as the driver has breakfast, the fumes assaulting the fresh air. As it pulls away, I am left alone to absorb one of the most moving of the Camino's many special places.

The Cruz dominates the crest of the hill, the highest point of the Camino. The landscape below is bathed in pale morning light; an altar cloth of woodland and fields.

The pictures in guidebooks are no preparation for the emotion of standing beneath this ancient symbol of release. For a while I sit at the base of the huge cairn amongst the stones, examining a few decorated with drawings or marked with names. The mound is three metres tall and spreads over a large area, it is hard to say where the cairn ends and the car parks begin. Millions of feet have made numerous tracks that lead up the mini mountain from the base of the cairn to the pole in the centre. People have not only left stones to form the cairn, they have also jammed them into the cracks in the wooden pole, alongside bits of paper and colourful fragments of cloth; little scraps of sad or hopeful hearts from all over the world. Small wooden blocks painted with messages have also been nailed to the post. There are plastic toys, mini statues, and traditional Christian medals. So many yearnings and meanings are gathered around this landmark, each one with its own story, and my bag of memories will join them. Spread out on a picnic table they look like the bits and pieces from the kitchen drawer of life. Each object has been chosen with such thought; it must be given due respect. They include a small cloth bag of mementos for a much-loved son and brother who died alone of a heart attack in his bed, stricken by grief and alcoholism after the death of his wife from cancer. A pebble of rose quartz symbolises the love a friend has for her ageing parents who are both suffering from dementia. A moonstone, a symbol of clarity, hope and new beginnings, is for my parents for all that they gave me, and another for a sister who died in infancy. I will put a small cross in the stones for all my wonderful Irish uncles and aunts, people I shall never forget. Then I will place the shells, fronds from the spruce tree and personal notes for my relative who is now at peace. There are a few more stones, gems and trinkets from friends who have no religious leanings, but who want to mark a personal meaning on an ancient cairn they will never visit.

It is traditional to throw the token onto the pile and say the Cruz de Ferro prayer: 'O Lord, may the stone which I bring to this holy place be a sign of pilgrimage to Santiago. When I reach my final judgment, tip the balance of my life in favour of my good deeds. I lay down this token which I carry from my home.' It is a simple and beautiful petition. Others I carry up to the pole and hang them on a wire stretched around its diameter. It takes me an hour to carry out a mini ritual for each memory, and all the while I have this towering symbol to myself, the sun rising ever higher. And then, tears fall for all the sorrows piled high here, inner hurts which rarely get a chance to see the light.

The Cruz de Ferro is the most obvious of the Camino's gathering places, it has drawn people from the world over to take part in a collective ritual that defines the essence of what this pilgrimage is about; a place to pause, to remember what matters, to celebrate, to be grateful, to acknowledge pain, and what is helped by being placed on the ground. It touches everyone who makes their way here with humility, whether a pilgrim or not, but perhaps especially if a pilgrim. In the film *The Way*, the scene at the Cruz de Ferro is one of the most moving as the characters lay down their own burdens – a lost son, an abusive marriage, a lack of self-worth, a writer who cannot write. My offerings and those of family and friends have disappeared into this mass of longing. They are indistinguishable from all the other shards of hearts that have been left to withstand the heat, rain and snow. Every single one of them is important. I don't know what happens to this great pile of stuff, whether it is periodically reduced to make way for new stones, or if it just gets higher and higher. It doesn't matter. For as long as

they are allowed to remain my memories will sit at the foot
of a cross as part of a pilgrimage in a time of plague.

The power of the Cruz is captured by the iron cross, I
doubt it would work if a statue or another symbol sat on
the top of the pole. A cross has a meaning that speaks
beyond the shape, it is the simplest and most ancient of
designs that was in use way before Christianity. It is created
by two straight lines placed one across the other such that
the ratio naturally pleases the eye. A cross can mirror the
shape of the human body with arms outstretched, or it can
be purely symmetrical and equal in all aspects. Our brains
are hard-wired to appreciate the inherent balancing of
dimensions and forces in a cross, it is a satisfying and
comfortable design. The intersection draws our attention
to a vanishing point, suggesting a meeting of divergent
paths. Variations of the cross have been used as symbols for
as long as we have written records.

The ankh, where the top of the vertical arm of the
cross is a loop, is an Ancient Egyptian symbol of life. It
was placed over the heart or on the lips of the dead as a
key to the door to the afterlife. The oval shape at the top
and the straight line of the lower vertical have sexual
connotations that represent reproduction and the cycle of
life. The combination of straight and curved lines also
indicates a balance of opposites, a harmony in the universe
that nurtures life. Today it has been adopted as a symbol of
African cultural identity, pagan beliefs and goth subculture.
The ankh is as rich in meaning now as when it first
appeared in hieroglyphics 3,000 years ago.

The cross known as the swastika was similarly life-
enhancing but was bastardised in the twentieth century. The
original word is from the ancient Indian language of Sanskrit
and meant well-being, and used for millennia by Hindus,
Buddhists and Jains to symbolise purity, peace and harmony.

Western travellers to Asia were so inspired by its simplicity and positive messaging that by the beginning of the twentieth century swastikas were adopted as a symbol by Coca Cola™, Carlsberg™ and the Boy Scouts. The Girls Club in America called their magazine *Swastika* and used a swastika badge as a prize. It was only when German academics latched onto old Indian texts that referred to 'fair-skinned foreign invaders' called Aryans coming from the north to overpower the dark-skinned races that the symbol soured. An imagined shared ancestry with the Aryans created the vile fantasy of white, superior, god-like warriors. The black, hooked-armed *hakenkreuz* (hooked cross) was placed on the distinctive white circle and red background of the Nazi flag, and it became inextricably linked to the atrocities committed under the Third Reich. In the West, the swastika transitioned from a symbol of well-being to one of hate.

The fact that two lines can be so laden with associations, both good and bad, is proof that our high-functioning brains utilise far more than words alone can convey. Plain symbols can hide immense complexity, and nowhere is that more obvious than at the Cruz de Ferro.

Hand-made crosses are scattered amongst the stones, echoing the one towering above. They are less permanent than the rocks, mostly made from twigs from the nearby forest. These cross mementos are not unique to the Cruz, hand-made crosses are found right across the Camino and appear in the most surprising of places. Needing no more than two sticks or two pieces of grass stem, people have woven them into fences, laid them at the side of roads, propped them up in windowsills or placed them amongst the rubble of ruins. In Navarre, a utilitarian wire fence close to a main highway is covered in hand-made crosses that are anonymous, random, and cobbled together into a piece of participatory art, a collaboration between strangers. They have turned a safety fence into a public art installation. The result is an organic, woody, grassy tapestry that shields the walker from the thundering traffic beyond. As I passed by it many weeks ago, I left my own contribution to blocking out the road. There is something special about crude, heartfelt, authentic offerings. They are wordless statements that are more substance than style, a shorthand that is instinctively understood. Undoubtedly, some symbols gain more power for being battered and simple.

That night it is very cold, and I stay in the only bed and breakfast in El Acebo, a small village halfway down the mountain. The pre-dawn sky is cloudless. A marbled moon throws a silvery shroud over the garden below, the mountain range beyond is black and forbidding. Venus is shining with a painful intensity. Named after the Roman god of love and beauty, the steady presence of Venus had accompanied us through the most turbulent of days last month in England, piercing the darkness with steady light; it was a source of comfort. This morning, though, and without warning, the awfulness of that time hits me with a force I am not prepared for. The scene is no longer beautiful. Venus glares down as a cold reminder of the finality of death. A lifeless planet hangs over a tragic human one, and it is too much. The cloud of horror barely lifts all day, despite the brilliant sunshine and the splendour of the landscapes.

I first spot him a few days later, in the middle of farmland. He has been watching me for a while, waiting on a bench for me to catch up. I can't tell how old he is, maybe 40, Spanish, friendly and travelling alone. He tells me I must be the lone, female pilgrim he keeps hearing about. We walk together, and at first it is a pleasant change to have company, but something isn't quite right. He tells me this is the fourth time he has walked the Camino this year. For most people, once or twice in a lifetime is enough, so why so many? His answer makes my heart sink. It is not that he wants to keep walking, he says, but he has no choice, God is asking him to. He tells me he has been given a special gift and as a devout Catholic he must obey his calling. He says he knows his mission is very important. I don't ask what the mission is, or his special gift, but I know I will find out. After a while, when we stop to fill water bottles, he takes out a large plastic bag full of small silver medals embossed with the Virgin Mary, the kind people give to children as a token on their First Holy Communion. He hands me one and tells me to always carry it with me for protection, I need it, he says ominously, more than I can possibly know.

That night, we are the only two people in a beautiful albergue in Villafranca del Bierzo, it creaks and sighs like an old lady. Did I realise, he says over dinner in the kitchen, that I am full of demons? They are literally swarming around me like flies around a carcass (my embellishment, he didn't make that exact analogy, but it is what he meant). No, I didn't know that, but I'm not surprised, I joke, trying to keep it light. Honestly, they are harmless, and we get on well together, don't worry about them, they're quite friendly. I constantly turn the conversation away from evil spirits to the weather, Covid, my family at home in Bristol, and how much I am looking forward to seeing them again – anything but devils. An ancient, empty albergue is not a good place to be trapped with a religious fantasist who has his eyes fixed on your demons. I retire to the dormitory early and choose a bunk at the far end of the room and pretend to be asleep when he comes in. Through a half-open eye I watch him neatly lay out his things, smoothing his clothes and placing them in perfectly straight lines on a bed. He then kneels to pray.

Just down the hill sits the Church of Santiago with its famous Puerta del Perdón, the Door of Forgiveness, a thirteenth-century portal that pilgrims could pass through to receive a special papal blessing that absolved them from their sins. For many sick and injured travellers who would not make it to Santiago, this was the equivalent of going to the actual cathedral of St James, giving the town the name, Little Santiago. Here they received their stamp of honour as though they had completed the whole pilgrimage and they could die in peace, knowing their efforts had been recognised. A visit to the Door of Forgiveness and a special absolution might be needed tomorrow if the demon slayer doesn't back off.

He stays with me for the next couple of days, insisting my devilish companions must be expelled before more harm is done. I have so many, he says, at times it is hard to look at me. This gives me a glimmer of hope that he might find my company too much. He tells me he can exorcise them, but only if I want him to. It won't work if I don't want him to. I don't want him to. He tells me he has done it many times before and people are transformed and made whole. I still don't.

At Las Herrerías, the only place open is a bar-come-hostel. I book a single room and so does he. There is a change in the weather and snow is falling. At first it dusts, and then coats the roofs of the empty houses and the car-less road. It is beautiful to watch the snowflakes drifting through the streetlights, swirling in the wind. More and more snow falls, and everywhere becomes silent and white. Tomorrow is a long, steep climb out of Castile y León and into Galicia, to the well-known and ancient village of O Cebreiro at the top of a ridge. I devise a plan; I will spend two nights there in the hope the demon slayer will move on and get a day ahead of me. I relax just a little and look out of the window at a disappearing world.

The following morning the Camino path is blocked by snow and impossible to follow, there is no alternative but to walk along the main road to O Cebreiro, which sits at 1,300m. The morning light is grey, and the sky shares the same washed-out, grey whiteness. The mountain-top village is deep in snow and by late afternoon it is falling once again in heavy, swirling flakes. I check into a lovely warm room with a view across the village square. It is Christmas-card white, and snowdrifts are forming against the stone walls of the famous round houses and the ancient church. No one is outside and there are no footprints to break the surface. Large icicles hang from roofs, dagger-sharp. It feels like Narnia. That evening I tell the demon slayer I am staying another night and he confirms he will carry on. The second day is even colder and snowier and sadly, as it is a weekend, my room had already been booked. I am forced to leave the warmth for another hotel which is twice the price and freezing cold. Even wearing all my warm clothes and inside a sleeping bag, I can't keep warm. Cold has infiltrated the fabric of the building and the owner refuses to put on the heating; but at least I am alone.

The church is quiet and calm, and I light a candle which throws a soft light against the stone wall. Another famous Camino miracle is said to have taken place here. Around 1300, a poor, devout farmer struggled through a blizzard (much like the one today) to reach the church for mass. The weather was so poor he was late, but the pompous priest told him off in front of the congregation. At the blessing of the bread and wine it is said that blood dripped onto the altar cloth and the head of the statue of the Virgin Mary turned to look at the chalice. The priest was filled with remorse at his cold-heartedness and the peasant was exonerated. They are both buried in the church in simple tombs. Another day, another miracle of weirdness and hope to confound a logical world. The demon slayer told me he loves this historical account and often sits for hours by the altar where it is said to have happened. Apparently, once a year, the relic of dried blood becomes real. I find that too macabre to contemplate and wander the snow-deep, narrow streets, buy a pair of warm socks and look out over the mountains through a blizzard of white flakes.

It is now the second week of December. The next day the trees and bushes are laden with snow and a heavy frost makes the world glisten like a glitter-covered Christmas card. It is lunchtime by the time I leave O Cebreiro. I can't face a long walk and plan to stop a few miles down the road.

The wind had picked up overnight and it is blowing strongly, walking into it is difficult and painful. Hail and snow hit my face, forcing me to squint and retreat into my hood as far as I can. On the crest of a hill a large, bronze statue of St Roque shows he too is battling the gale. One hand holds onto his pilgrim hat, the other is driving his staff into the ground as he strides forwards, his cloak billowing behind him. The two of us are alone on this wild, wintry summit; our clothes are covered in snow and both of us have turned our faces against the wind. He looks as embattled as me. Snow is piling up around his feet, and mine, so I move on. I like St Roque, he was a good man in the dangerous times of the fourteenth century, and he was another saint who cared about animals.

St Roque is often depicted lifting his tunic to show a large, weeping sore on his thigh, a sign of the bubonic plague. He usually has a dog at his side, which is carrying a loaf of bread. Legend has it that Roque was a French nobleman who gave away his wealth to the poor, much like St Francis 200 years earlier. He was famous for tending to victims of the plague, and when he contracted it himself, he retreated to the forest to die alone. Every day a dog visited him, bringing bread and licking his sores clean. When he eventually recovered, which was rare for the plague, he returned to his original home in Montpellier. By then, the city was at war and Roque was thrown into prison for doing good, something the authorities considered suspicious. He died in a dungeon five years later. His refusal to be saved by allowing people to know of his noble birth led him to being canonised. The Catholic Church now regards him as the patron saint of dogs, dog owners, knee problems, surgeons, the infirm, bachelors, diseased cattle, and against cholera, plague, skin rashes, contagious diseases, pestilence and epidemics. That is quite a list. Before I leave St Roque to the mountain storm, I offer a prayer to him for all those afflicted by the terrible twenty-first-century epidemic that is racing across the globe, killing thousands and causing untold suffering and heartache.

The village of Fonfría comes into view as the light fades, and two dogs rush at me from a farm. They look like they mean business and I have to use my poles to fend them off. At a distant whistle, they retreat. The albergue is not much further on, and once again I am the only one staying. The room is simple but warm and the owner welcoming and provides a supper, then leaves. The feeling of loneliness and the weirdness of the past couple of days is deadening. Throughout the night the wind moans around the windows and the dogs bark relentlessly in the distant farmyard. I send another request to St Roque to ask him to throw a blanket over them, they must be so bitterly cold. At times, snow crashes to the ground from the roof, a loud thud which jolts me awake. There are about seven days to go until I reach Santiago, it is almost within touching distance. Galicia is the final province, and it feels like the home straight of a marathon. The weather has changed, the scenery is changing by the day and my mood is shifting to accommodate the end of a long and strange journey. I can't tell if I am glad or sad.

CHAPTER TEN

Ultreia

Stars glitter in the sky and along the trail. Small, flat, shiny plates of mica flash from walls and footpaths. Mica is a mineral common in rocks that have been altered by intense geological processes. The surface of the earth is not static; the vast shifting plates can be dragged to great depths, miles beneath the surface. Sediments that were laid down in oceans, rivers, fertile plains and deserts are metamorphosed – reconstituted, and altered in form and identity. When they surface millions of years later, they are often transformed beyond recognition. That is what I see now lining the track of the Camino: glittery metamorphic rocks, and mica glinting in the morning sun. It is true, sometimes beautiful things result from a journey through prolonged heat and pressure. Galicia is founded on many such rocks, and they are used to construct buildings and laid as paving stones to form roads. The Way of St James, often referred to as the Path of the Milky Way, leads to St James of the Starry Meadow and it is paved with tiny, mineral stars.

Upland Galician villages are less cosy and communal than in other regions, they are strung out with no central square and they emit a stoic independence. Dogs are always barking – everywhere, every day there is barking; it seems every house has a barking dog. Small, old-fashioned farms line the paths of this gritty region, complete with stables, haylofts and chickens. As I watch an old man mending farm machinery, a sheep peers out of one door, a cow from another, hens look down from roof beams and a dog sits patiently at his heels. Later the same afternoon, doe-eyed, breathy, gentle cows walk home along a narrow road, they creak and sway as they pass by. A farmer follows behind and he nods; it is a meditative, end-of-day scene. I notice he has an umbrella hanging down his back, suspended from the collar of his coat.

Atlantic winds carry rain across this Celtic corner of Spain. Prehistoric monuments are scattered through the landscape; just under the surface, ancient languages murmur incantations from another time. Myriad small fields are defined by drystone walls laid by hands who knew and understood the balance of rocks and their footbed of soil; they shelter vegetables being grown for the local, warming stews. The change in atmosphere is palpable. This is a different land, more akin to the west of Ireland, Wales or Cornwall than anywhere else along the Camino. Here, pre-Christian gods sit alongside crucifixes, and they both claim the land as their own.

At Triacastela, the less-travelled, alternative route looks more appealing than the main Camino footpath, which follows the Oribio river. The track climbs a hill before descending into the major Camino town of Sarria. Snow still covers the ground, and it gets deeper as I climb. The wind has been strong here, evidenced by the limbs of trees, even whole trunks, which lie across the footpath. At first I keep going, clambering over and under the tangle of branches and plodding through the snowdrifts, but it is getting harder to make progress. At times it takes me a good 10 minutes to get over one fallen tree by throwing my rucksack to the other side before trying to find a way through for myself. The sky is threatening more sleet and snow, it is cold and I am soaked to the skin and dripping with sweat. The top of the hill is still a long way in the distance and is shrouded in cloud. Eventually, I give up, it is foolish and stubborn to keep going on my own, and I am angry at my poor judgement and the waste of time. The fortunes of a trip can turn in an instant – on an infected blister, a sprained ankle, on bad planning, on an honest mistake, on a stupid decision. Being alone on a snowy hillside, separated from anyone else by a path blocked by fallen trees, is a recipe for disaster. Determination is one thing; blind bloody-mindedness is another. It is a character trait I keep trying to correct, not always with success.

Diary entry: Mammoth Lakes, California, September 2017

Pre-dawn over Thousand Island Lake, perhaps the most beautiful part of the John Muir Trail. Towering mountains were perfectly mirrored in the silent, still water. A long day of strenuous walking lay ahead and I was already tired and suffering from the altitude. My plan was to get off the trail for a night and stay in Mammoth Lakes, a bustling, bright town-come-ski-resort; I knew I needed to regroup and restock, and to get my head together for the mountains ahead. As the day wore on, I started to make mistakes, I missed turnings and wandered off track. It was increasingly hard to concentrate. I wasn't drinking or eating enough and I could feel myself losing touch. After 12 miles or so a soft green campsite appeared, right by a river. It was tempting to call it a day, it was mid-afternoon and another tent was already pitched there. A man was cooking over a fire, he looked up and smiled in welcome. I had enough food for another couple of days, there was plenty of space and it was a sensible time to stop – but I was determined to press on. Miles went by through burnt-out forests, the result of wildfires a few years earlier, the sandy tracks were hard work, there were steep ascents and descents. Quite quickly I ran out of water. Eventually, I was on the outskirts of a well-known tourist attraction, Devils Postpile, but I couldn't find the right trail, there were signs pointing in all directions but none of them seemed to match my map. More people were around now, day-trippers exploring the forests and rock formations, but no one made any sense when I asked them directions. I was verging on delirious. I was trying to find a bus stop to catch a lift into town and I knew I was close, but I ended up walking two miles down a track to a dead end and had to retrace my steps and start again. By now it was almost dark, my nose started to bleed and I was very thirsty. All of a sudden, a track through some trees emptied me into a car park with a queue of holiday makers waiting for the bus. People glanced at me strangely, God knows what I looked like. One kind woman approached me with a bottle of water, 'Do you need this, honey?' The bus arrived and it was standing room only. I must have looked terrible as someone gave me their seat. The lady next to me was concerned.

'Are you OK, hun?'

'I will be, thanks.'

'Can I ask what you're doing? You don't look great.'

'Walking from Yosemite to Mount Whitney.'

'On your own?'

'Yes.'

She stared.

'But why?'

I didn't know how to answer that and closed my eyes.

By the time the bus got to Mammoth Lakes it was dark. The atmosphere was festive and people everywhere were singing, shouting, drinking. I asked the bus driver to point me in the direction of budget hotels and he looked at me with astonishment. 'You do have a reservation, right? You know it's Labor-Day weekend? This resort is jam-packed, lady.'

For another hour I dragged myself from one hotel/ motel to another, but nowhere had a room. Even the campsite on the outskirts of town was full. I stood in the middle of the busiest, brightest street in town, with cars rushing past and partying people spilling out onto the pavement and felt lonelier than I have ever felt in my life. At the next place I tried the receptionist just laughed when I asked if there was anything at all I could stay in, even a broom cupboard. She shook her head, the resort had been booked out for weeks. The last motel had a long, steep drive. A big sign in the window shouted 'NO VACANCIES'. I stood in the doorway, leaning against the frame, and waited for the receptionist to put the phone down.

'Please, tell me your sign isn't true.'

'Ma'am you have the love of God on your side, that call was a last-minute cancellation. I reckon you just got the last room in town.'

I told him I loved him.

What did I learn from that, other than sometimes, luck can fall from the stars just when you are about to give in? Yet again, I came face to face with my stubborness, lack of preparation and naivety. I lay in my room, barely able to move. My plan had pulled off – but only just – and through no skill on my part. If this piece of luck hadn't materialised, I would have been uncomfortable but fine, I would have spent a cold night in a bus shelter or found a patch of grass to pitch my tent, but further into the trail or on a mountain, would a lack of planning be more serious?

That night I watched an American documentary on Alex Honnold, the legendary climber who had taken the world by storm. Just weeks earlier, at the age of 33, he had broken all records and solo climbed the sheer 2,300m wall of rock called El Capitan, which looms above the Yosemite Valley, an unbelievable feat of athleticism, courage and skill. Not long ago I had lain in my tent and stared in awe at its vertical granite face stark against the

stars, huge and imposing. Honnold took a mere three
hours to reach the top; some of the earliest attempts with
teams of men and ropes took three days. Honnold was
the first to climb El Capitan with no safety support of
any kind. Watching him is a dizzying, heart-stopping
spectacle – a small, fragile body suspended high above the
ground in the middle of a vast sheet of rock, with only
the tiniest finger-holes and ridges between him and
death. At times, it is too hard to watch.

The documentary showed him preparing by climbing
different sections of the route with the help of friends
and ropes; it was a masterclass in mindfulness. Every move
was in the moment, planned and thoughtful. The position
of every hold, each twist and turn of his body, was mapped
and stored in his head, and then drawn out on paper and
memorised. He executed a detailed plan and never took
risks. His stock response to everyone's question about the
obvious mortal danger: 'If I thought I was going to die, I
wouldn't do it.' He knows precisely what he is doing at
every second he is on a rock face.

Feeling humbled, I decided to be more Honnold, less
Colwell, to think things through with more care, to be
knowledgeable at every turn in the road. Sometimes it
works, but not always.

The lower, less snowy but mushier route took me to
Sarria, a Roman town that marks the starting point for
half of the pilgrims walking the Camino. To get the
coveted Compostela stamp, the official recognition of
completion, you must have walked the last 100km, which
is the distance from Sarria to Santiago de Compostela. It
is strange how that doesn't seem far now, but it isn't a
gentle, downhill stroll to the end. The vast, quiet plains
and the forested mountains seem a long way back, but
there are still hills and dales ahead.

By this time, I am as battered and weary as an old war horse. Sitting on a rock making tea one morning, a young couple walk past, fresh as daisies from their start in Sarria. They trot like antelopes down the path, their scallop shells swinging from their packs. Their boots are clean and there is no mud on their trousers. I feel self-conscious and ragged. My tiny scallop pin-badge fell off my waist-belt a long time ago.

Away from the transhumance farms of hilly Galicia, the scenery becomes a mixture of intensive dairy farming, eucalyptus plantations, increasing urbanisation and industrialisation; a sense of edging closer to the modern world and all that it brings. At one village a thin, soggy, hungry kitten meows loudly and tries to curl around my feet. No houses seem occupied, there is no one obvious to take care of it, so I feed it some tortilla, which it devours, and the end of a carton of milk, which it drinks without pause. It follows me for a long way down the track. The weather continues to challenge with heavy rain, and I cut an isolated figure in a woodland clearing as it pelts off my rucksack and bounces off a picnic table. I try to eat a sandwich, but the bread is too dry in contrast to the water all around. The woodland is predominantly eucalyptus, which infuses the air with its astringent oil, made more intense by the dampness. Piles of felled, stripped trunks line the path, their long, stringy fronds of bark scattered all around.

I carried to my lips a spoonful of the tea in which I had let soften a bit of madeleine. But at the very instant when the mouthful of tea mixed with cake crumbs touched my palate, I quivered, attentive to the extraordinary thing that was happening inside me.

The famous passage from Marcel Proust's 1913 novel, *À la recherche du temps perdu*, describes the intense experience when smell and taste trigger a rush of memories and set the mind reeling. It pinpoints this common sensory experience so well that it has been given its own name, the Proustian moment. In Proust's case it was crumbs of cake in tea, but any taste and smell can form a lightning rod to the past.

Smell is an underrated human sense, working in the background of our consciousness like a puppeteer pulling the strings of our emotions. Through smell we get an invisible indication of the world and its dangers, and not only what is food, what is not. Smell tells us about people, about someone's age, emotional state, health, even their mating potential. A myriad of smells drift through the air of our everyday life, laden with messages that we barely register, but we heed them nonetheless. In the past, so vital was a good sense of smell to staying alive, evolution finely honed our noses to be an exquisitely sensitive organ.

Air thick with the smell of eucalyptus oil took me back to living in Australia, to lying under a red river gum on a hot day watching a restless flycatcher dart about the branches. The shade cast by the long, thick branches, the quality of the light filtered through olive-coloured leaves, the hushed contentedness, the heat shimmer above the red earth, all of it came back. The red gum was a grand old specimen; a strong, steady presence in a strong and steady landscape. Its roots went deep to find water, its pale bark could withstand frequent fires, its shade sheltered many creatures from intense sunlight; it performed its ecological function with aplomb. The tree was where it was meant to be. But in our highly managed world, the right tree in the right place is not guaranteed.

The first record of eucalyptus in Spain was in 1863. Rosendo Salvado, a missionary monk, sent seeds from Australia to his family in Pontevedra, a town 60km south of Santiago. Ten years later the demand for fuel and for wooden supports in mines, drove the establishment of plantations across the country. Seeds also began to disperse naturally, displacing native trees in the wild. Today, eucalyptus is the most abundant tree species in Galicia, seeing a 14-fold increase in 50 years from 28,000 hectares in 1973 to nearly 400,000 hectares in 2021.

The spread of eucalyptus plantations has coincided with increasing global temperatures and the associated escalation in wildfires across Europe. Devastating incendiaries cause loss of crops, natural habitats, people's homes, businesses, livestock, wildlife and human life. Although most fires seem to have been started by people, either through accident or design, once underway they are more deadly than in the past. Counter-intuitively, rain-soaked Galicia has become a wildfire hotspot, with almost 40 per cent of the fires in Spain breaking out here between 2001 and 2015. In 2020, more acreage was burned than in the last two years combined. As eucalyptus is naturally highly flammable, an adaptation to Australia's fire-prone environment, some people believe their presence is making a bad situation worse. Lack of management of forests and continuing land abandonment as people leave farming are also contributory factors, but few disagree that eucalyptus plantations are not good news in a hotter, drier Spain.

The end of the trail, the cathedral at Santiago de Compostela, is now just a couple of days away. As I emerge out of a tunnel of bushes, the demon slayer is standing by the side of the road; I have caught him up and there is no alternative but to walk together. A defined track may be a good thing, but it does mean there is nowhere to hide. I console myself that this is an authentic pilgrimage experience; meeting religious fanatics must have been common in medieval times when religion was

far more heightened than it is today. Dreading an evening
of demon talk I evoke a blessing from St Julian, a favourite
saint in Galicia and the patron saint of travellers journeying
far from home and hoping to find safe lodgings.

As ever, the stories surrounding the fourth-century
Julian are varied, but in essence, they all revolve around
him killing his parents in a case of rage and mistaken
identity. This terrible prophecy was given by a deer he
was hunting (or a witch in the woods, depending on the
version), and which he had tried very hard to stop being
realised. Fate, though, cannot be outwitted. Even though
he left France to travel to Galicia to avoid contact with
them, after many years his parents came to find him. He
was out hunting when they arrived at his home, and his
wife let them rest in their bed until he returned. Not
realising what had happened and assuming his wife was in
bed with a lover, Julian flew into a rage and killed them as
they slept. When he saw his wife happily cooking dinner
he realised what he had done and was so filled with
remorse he became a helper of pilgrims on the Camino
as a penance. The legend tells us that years later a poor
leper came to his hospital who was desperately ill and on
the verge of death. As Julian comforted him in his final
hours, the man suddenly rose up, shining with light and
beauty, and told Julian that because of his good actions his
sins were now forgiven. Julian was later canonised and
became associated with travellers looking for safe hostels.

I shall miss these strange stories, the half-mythical, half-
remembered fables of half-real characters who morphed
through time and the telling of the tale. At their core they
express a deep-seated need to acknowledge human weakness
and put right past wrongs. I shall also miss the sense of
continuity with ancestors who faced troubling times long
ago. There are many small chapels and crosses devoted to St

Julian across Galicia, often on the remains of much older sites dedicated to Roman gods of roads and travellers. Even rivers and pools which were once homes of pagan gods, are now sacred Christian waters. Sadly, St Julian didn't answer my petition and the demon slayer and I end up sharing lodgings and the trail for the final stages to Santiago.

The last day dawns with sublime beauty. Early-morning mist hovers over the fields laid out beneath a pink sky. There is an air of closure, of coming together, of arriving. The demon slayer had spent the previous evening telling me he thought my demons were calmer than when we first met, he felt the Camino had done me good.

Rarely do plans work out as imagined. My dream of walking into the cathedral square and being alone with my thoughts evaporates with the morning mist. I had wanted the final day to be just me, but as we are the only two people in the accommodation, we pack up and head out for the cathedral city.

It is a surprisingly long, hilly slog to Santiago, or perhaps I am tired. More eucalyptus plantations separate more intensive farmland, but the discovery of a devil's finger fungus is a light moment. Originally from the southern hemisphere, it is thought to have arrived in Europe in 1914 with supplies for World War I, and it is as creepy as mushrooms get. The fungi spend much of their time underground, feeding on rotting vegetation. When it is time to reproduce, they appear on the surface as gelatinous, golf ball sized 'eggs'. When these burst they reveal bright red tentacles covered in foul-smelling patches of greenish-black slime, like a bloodied hand reaching out of the earth. I tell the demon slayer that the devil is trying to grab us and drag us into the depths, but he isn't amused. To make matters worse, a little further on is the decayed body of a viper, which is too far gone to identify. I comment on the disrespect Christianity has shown to these amazing creatures, and he eyes me suspiciously and gives the snake a wide berth. His medieval mind inhabits his weird world with signs and symbols.

Close to Santiago the trail passes through the village of Lavacolla on the banks of the Sionlla River. Today, it is a modern town in the shadow of Santiago airport, but in earlier days it provided what must have been a much-needed service, the last chance for pilgrims to wade into the river and perform a ritual cleansing before entering the holy city. The *Codex Calixtinus* calls it by its old name, Lavamentula. There is debate about what happened here, all of them to do with washing. Some say it is the place where pilgrims washed their genitals as a sign of respect to St James, before arriving at his tomb. Others believe it was for a general wash and brush-up. Strangely, women were excused. It gives an indication of the state that most pilgrims must have been in, especially as prostitutes were increasingly common close to the city. Some modern pilgrims still swim in the river's much-reduced flow, especially in the summer months, probably more for the benefits of wild swimming than genital cleansing, but it wasn't enticing in December.

The end of all the various Camino routes is Santiago's Praza do Obradoiro (Square of the Workshop) to face the towering façade of the Catedral de Santiago. Usually, the square is full of emotional pilgrims offloading their backpacks and absorbing what it means to have arrived. Thousands time their arrival to attend the famous pilgrim's mass. Most go straight into the cathedral to bask in religious grandeur and to stand at the tomb of St James. In normal years, the square would be a place of comings and goings, a jumbled confusion of the religious, the spiritual, the commercial and the curious. Today, though, is not normal, today falls in the middle of a global pandemic, and the only people in the square are me, the demon slayer and three very drunk Irish men, singing and swearing loudly. The demon slayer hovers in the background, shifting from one foot to the other, waiting and watching – always watching. I turn my back on him, sit on the ground and close my eyes; I want to shut this dystopian world out of my head.

It is suddenly over. There is a sense of relief to have made it, of completion and accomplishment, but there is also an overwhelming feeling of longing which has no specific focus. There is no one to hug, no one to share the moment with, no one to exchange wordless acknowledgement. Nor is there any closure within the cathedral walls, it is locked and boarded up, it is not even possible to get a glimpse of the inside. Covid and restorations have surrounded the gothic masterpiece with plastic sheeting and wooden boards, and cranes tower above. There is no pilgrim's mass for spiritual expression, and no *botafumeiro*, the giant incense burner that swings above the heads of the crowd gathered below; its fragrant smoke represents prayers ascending to heaven, but in the past, it also sweetened the air infused with body odour. There is no contemplation by the remains of a personal friend of Jesus of Nazareth, a man whose bones caused stars to fall from the heavens. The cathedral has no room for pilgrims in this shattered world, we are shut out. On this mid-December day in 2020 there is just a small miscellany of humanity gathered on the outside, most of it drunk, and we are barred from entering the sanctuary. There is something symbolic about that. But none of it matters.

The extraordinary thing is that this pilgrimage continues to work a thousand years after its humble beginnings in a remote meadow lit by the Milky Way. It may have changed to become far less religious and far more diffuse than for most of its history. It still is, though, a unique and memorable encounter with the human condition. It is why the ancient tales and wondrous miracles continue to speak to the modern mind. A hedge fund manager on a twenty-first-century Camino can as easily be brought to tears by standing at the site of a miracle or in front of a piece of Camino art, or by an unexpected act of kindness, as any poor, medieval pilgrim in a cloak and sandals. And what of the next thousand years? Will St James keep his power of attraction? I believe so; thousands will still want to walk its many paths, and every single one will be a unique journey of meaning. In my notes, which I write in the albergue on the last night, I ask myself three questions:

Is this a medieval circus that plays on a sentimentality for the past? Yes.

Is it a commercial venture that exploits the desire for meaning, the image of saints and the bizarreness of miracles? Yes.

Is it worth doing? YES.

I scribble down a further question: Has walking the Camino Francés helped me cope with a world in turmoil? That is less easy to answer. Time taken to reflect is never wasted, but there have been no blinding solutions or insights, if anything only more questions. But definitive answers can't be the point – if only it were that easy. The biggest contribution has been the filling of a spiritual tank running on empty, of glimpsing a sense of perspective on present troubles that only a thousand years of history can provide, of tentatively reconnecting with a global religion whose institutional structure I want to love more than I do. The Camino was there when I needed it, it provided delight alongside the doubt and confusion, and it allowed a slow gathering.

Walking the Camino is being open to the mysterious and the uncontrollable, to feeling exposed, to accepting what it means to be one tiny part of an immensity. It is at once both vast and kaleidoscopic, allowing space to contemplate eternity alongside the minutiae of every day. In today's sceptical, even cynical, age the Camino is a safe space where no one questions or judges your motives. As the journey progresses, the exoskeleton of ego crumbles into the dusty tracks to expose the vulnerability of a soft-bodied human in a chaotic world, no doubt a feeling shared with the earliest pilgrims. Walking a pathway of meaning, religious or not, answers a deeply human need to explore both an inner and an outer landscape, and to realise they are inextricably linked. Amongst all the challenges, I felt held by something that is hard to define, and I now have a greater understanding of why pilgrimage is important to so many people.

For many modern pilgrims the end of the Camino isn't the cathedral; they carry on for a further 90km to Finisterre on the west coast. They go to see the sun rise over the sea and to get an inkling of what it was like to stand at what was once thought to be the literal end of the land, and hence its name. In days long ago, before the Christianisation of the route, people burned their clothes on the cliffs at Finisterre as a symbol of renewal. Now, swimming in the sea is the new purification. The real destination for many modern pilgrims is in nature, amongst rocks and wind and sea, away from the heavy ornateness of churches and their rules and judgements. I don't have time to walk on to Finisterre, and I am not sure I have the energy; I really want to go home. The cathedral square with its drunkards and a deluded religious fantasist marks the end of my strange pilgrimage.

After I text Maria, the taxi driver who helped me in Puente la Reina, and the kind hostel owner in La Virgen del Camino, the Camino begins to shut down and fold away. I no longer need the yellow arrows or scallop shell markers, or to fill any more water bottles. I am no longer on its pathways; it has taken me over 500 miles to the cathedral and its job is done. Done, but not finished, because what is replacing the way-marked trail is the sense that this is just a part of a much bigger journey for which there is no guidebook, which has no pre-described length and only a hazy sense of the final destination.

I leave for home on 13th December, an ancient marker in the calendar to celebrate the Winter Solstice, the Welsh Festival of Lights, *Gwyl o Golau*, and the feast day of St Lucy, the patron saint of light and clear vision. Lucy is my confirmation name, and I like to think of her walking by my side, raising her saintly lantern to help find the path ahead. But it is the old Camino greeting found in the *Codex* that will stick with me, the one I will take into the future. Not the usual 'Buen Camino', but the more ancient word of encouragement on a long journey, the one that recognises the effort it takes to reach a worthy destination – Ultreia. Don't give up, keep going, keep moving forwards – keep pushing through to the end.

Epilogue

The world has changed since I walked the Camino in 2020. The big events that dominated that time are still playing out, but some have shifted in focus. Covid is taking up less space, other crises are deepening.

At the time of writing, in December 2022, the pandemic has killed over 660 million people worldwide and rocked global economies. For the first time in many years there was a sense of collective effort to solve a planetary-wide crisis. The origin and spread of Covid increased our understanding of humanity's responsibility to the natural world and to each other, and it altered the concept of work and how it is carried out. All of us became more dependent on technology and we are now used to remote working and companionship, though loneliness was widespread, and despair increased as businesses went under in the lockdowns. Many families were stricken with grief, loss and isolation. The hardship brought to the surface an outburst of kindness, and a sense of community that had previously been buried under busyness.

Vaccinations against Covid were rolled out from 2021 and the pandemic slowly lost its grip. As it stands, face masks, social distancing and lockdowns are mainly a thing of the past in Europe, but many vulnerable people everywhere still live in fear.

Russia's invasion of Ukraine began in February 2022, a devastating war that is destroying lives and sending another shock wave through global economics, disrupting energy and food supplies. So far, there have been nearly 7,000 civilian deaths. Political and ideological fracture lines are deepening, and fear of world war simmers just beneath the surface.

The effects of climate change have intensified, 2022 was officially recognised as the warmest year on record for the

UK, with temperatures of over 40°C for the first time in recorded history. Wildfires raged at home and abroad. Between June and October, a third of Pakistan went underwater and nearly 2,000 people lost their lives, along with 700,000 livestock and vast swathes of crops. The world is hotter and experiencing more flooding, storms or drought. Ice caps and glaciers are melting at an unprecedented rate. The latest global meeting on tackling climate change, COP27, was held in November, who knows if any of the promises that were made to help developing countries cope with the damage will actually materialise. COP15, a similar gathering dedicated to reversing the terrifying loss of wildlife around the world, barely made the headlines.

There are good signs, too. Some hope for the Amazon rainforest surfaced as Jair Bolsonaro lost the presidential election in Brazil. Medical breakthroughs for Covid, cancer and Parkinson's disease became a reality. Incredible, mind-blowing images of space taken by the James Webb telescope were revealed, showing detailed, colourful pictures of black holes, nebulas, galaxies and planets. They show a dynamic, violent, restless universe that challenges every perception we have ever had that we are in charge. And the courageous women of Iran continue to defy oppression by demanding their right to freedom, although at great cost. They inspire us all. The human spirit is still strong.

These shafts of light illuminate a confusing picture of a world of smoking ruins and green shoots, and the enormity of it all can be overwhelming and at times, crushing. The deserted Camino with its long, empty pathways and sense of isolation and peace still lives within me; a well I can draw upon every day. I am deeply grateful for its complex messages and meanings, and they will continue to be a source of nourishment. Above all, I am eternally grateful for the opportunity to have walked a pilgrimage through these difficult, changing times.

Acknowledgements

I would like to thank Brian Clarke for help with the text, Alistair Dodd for his help with the Basque language, and Dr Nick Mayhew-Smith and Professor Tina Beattie for their kindness and wisdom. I could do nothing without the loving support of my family.

References and Further Reading

Chapter One: Wooden Staffs and Mountains

Camino de Santiago Forum. 2015. *The Relics of Sant Iago.* caminodesa ntiago.me/community/threads/the-relics-of-sant-iago.30614/

Johnson, R. U. 1916. *John Muir As I Knew Him.* Sierra Club. vault .sierraclub.org/john_muir_exhibit/life/johnson_tribute_scb_1 916.aspx

Mayhew-Smith, N. 2021. *Landscape Liturgies.* Nick Canterbury Press, Canterbury.

Picaud, A. *Codex Calixtinus.* Book V. codexcalixtinus.es/the-en glish-version-of-the-book-v-codex-calixtinus/

Scott, W. 1806. *Marmion.* Ed. H. Morley. Archibald Constable, Edinburgh.

Stanford, P. 2021. *Journey.* Thames and Hudson, London.

Turold. *c.*1090. *The Song of Roland,* stanza CXL, line 1861.

Walker, K. 2021. *Pilgrimages Could be the Next Post-COVID Travel Trend. National Geographic.* nationalgeographic.com/travel/artic le/could-pilgrimages-be-the-next-post-covid-travel-trend

Chapter Two: Moors and Myths

Gent, G. and Wilson, R. 1995. *The Flora of Northamptonshire and the Soke of Peterborough.* Robert Wilson Designs, Northampton.

Homily in the Reading of Scripture, 1547.

Jabr, F. 2014. *Why Walking Helps Us Think.* The *New Yorker.* newyorker. com/tech/annals-of-technology/walking-helps-us-think

Landsberg, S. 1996. *The Medieval Garden.* Thames and Hudson, London.

Putonen, E. *et al.* Quantification of Overnight Movement of Birch (*Betula pendula*) Branches and Foliage with Short Interval Terrestrial Laser Scanning. *Frontiers of Plant Science,* 29 February 2016, doi.org/10.3389/fpls.2016.00222.

Teale, E. W. ed. 1954. *The Wilderness World of John Muir*. Houghton
   Mifflin Company, Boston.

Chapter Three: Witches and Forests

Coelho, P. 1987. *The Pilgrimage*. Planeta Press, Madrid.

Conn, H. 2013. *Witches on The Way: Remember the Camino's
   Tarnished Halo*. Heather Conn Blogs. www.heatherconnblogs
   .com/witches-on-the-way/

Gimbel, L. M. 2012. 'Bawdy badges and the Black Death: late
   medieval apotropaic devices against the spread of the plague',
   (Thesis). Paper 497.

Gómez, J. M. and Verdú, M. 2017. Network theory may explain
   the vulnerability of medieval human settlements to the Black
   Death pandemic. *Scientific Reports* 7.

Henningsen, G., ed. 2004. The Instructions Issued by the Council
   for Dealing with Witchcraft Cases (Madrid, 29th August 1614),
   in *Salazar Documents: Inquisitor Alonso de Salazar Frias and Others
   on the Basque Witch Persecution*. Koninklijke Brill NV, Leiden.

Mackay, C. S. 2009. *The Hammer of Witches: A Complete Translation of
   the Malleus Maleficarum*. Cambridge University Press, Cambridge.

Mayhew-Smith, N. 2021. *Landscape Liturgies*. Canterbury Press,
   Norwich.

Muir, J. 1911. *The Mountain Trail and its Message*. Pilgrim Press.

Chapter Four: To the Stars

Picaud, A. *Codex Calixtinus*. Chapter 7. codexcalixtinus.es/the-en
   glish-version-of-the-book-v-codex-calixtinus/

The caption beneath a painting of Pan by Walter Crane.

Muir, J. 1911. *My First Summer in the Sierra*. Houghton Mifflin, Boston.

Chapter Five: The Kindness of Strangers

British Antarctic Survey. 2021. *Brunt Ice Shelf in Antarctica Calves*.
   bas.ac.uk/media-post/brunt-ice-shelf-in-antarctica-calves

Borotkanych, N. 2021. *The Year of 2020 in Satellite Highlights*. EOS Data Analytics. eos.com/blog/the-year-of-2020-in-satellite-hi ghlights

Camino de Santiago Forum. 2012. *Mystery of Obanos: English Saint Names?* caminodesantiago.me/community/threads/mystery-of -obanos-english-saint-names.13722/

Cassar, N. *et al.* 2021. Widespread phytoplankton blooms triggered by 2019–2020 Australian wildfires. *Nature.* 597: 370–375.

Cordis. 2021. *Promotion of rural museums and heritage sites in the vicinity of European pilgrimage routes.* cordis.europa.eu/project/id /101004887

Earnest, J. 2015. *Peter Schjeldahl with Jarrett Earnest.* The Brooklyn Rail. brooklynrail.org/2015/07/art/peter-schjeldahl-with-jarr ett-earnest

Green Pilgrimage. 2018. *Economic Impact of Pilgrims on St James Way.* projects2014-2020.interregeurope.eu/greenpilgrimage/news/ news-article/3616/economic-impact-of-pilgrims-on-st-james- way/

Illing, S. 2018. *Religion without God: Alain de Botton on "atheism 2.0."* Vox. vox.com/conversations/2016/10/6/13172608/reli gion-lent-atheism-christianity-god-alain-de-botton

Phillips, D. 2019. *Bolsonaro declares 'the Amazon is ours' and calls deforestation data 'lies'. The Guardian.* theguardian.com/world/2019 /jul/19/jair-bolsonaro-brazil-amazon-rainforest-deforestation

Statista. 2022. *Number of regular and irregular immigrants that arrived in Spain from 2015 to 2021.* statista.com/statistics/1214076/number -of-legal-and-illegal-immigrants-that-arrived-to-spain

Statista. 2022. *Number of deaths of irregular migrants entering Spain in 2020, by route of entry.* statista.com/statistics/1188843/irregular -migrants-dead-entering-spain-by-route

Velde, van der, I. R. *et al.* 2021. Vast CO_2 release from Australian fires in 2019–2020 constrained by satellite. *Nature.* 597: 366–369.

Vonnegut, K. 1965. *God Bless you Mr Rosewater.* Holt, Reinhart, Winston, Missouri.

Chapter Six: Wine and Wonder

Brown, P. 1981. *The Cult of Saints, its Rise and Function in Latin Christianity*. University of Chicago Press, Chicago.

Chesterton, G. K. 1927. *The Collected Poems of G. K. Chesterton*. Dodd Mead and Company, New York.

Picaud, A. *Codex Calixtinus*. Chapter 4. codexcalixtinus.es/the-english-version-of-the-book-v-codex-calixtinus/

Picaud, A. *Codex Calixtinus*. Chapter 6. codexcalixtinus.es/the-english-version-of-the-book-v-codex-calixtinus/

Chapter Seven: War and Peace

Brown, S. 2020. *The Way of St Francis*. Cicerone, Cumbria.

Ivask, I. 1983. Pivotal Places and Books as Travel Companions from Lapland to Cádiz and Cork, A.D. 1982. *World Literature Today*. 57: 383.

Kornfield, J. 1994. *Buddha's Little Instruction Book*. Bantam, New York.

Moratinos Life. 2007. *Bodega Land: Bilbo Doesn't Live Here Anymore*. moratinoslife.blogspot.com/2007/07/bodega-land-bilbo-doesnt-live-here.html

Moratinos Life. 2007. *Kinda Like Old Times*. moratinoslife.blogspot.com/2020/

SEO Birdlife. 2016. *El drama de los pájaros communes*. seo.org/2016/06/02/drama-los-pajaros-comunes/

Wordsworth, W. 1807. 'Nuns Fret Not At Their Convent's Narrow Room.'

Chapter Eight: The Unravelling Road

Kornfield, J. 1994. *Buddha's Little Instruction Book*. Bantam, New York.

Porter, M. 2016. *Grief is the Thing with Feathers*. Faber and Faber, London.

Chapter Nine: Stones and Snow

Mustich, J. 2020. *On Reading Graham Greene*. Medium. jamesmustich
.medium.com/on-reading-graham-greene-bc9e24ef523

Chapter Ten: Ultreia

Ecologistas en Acción. 2006. *Los incendios forestales en Galicia se
repiten año tras año*. ecologistasenaccion.org/5575/los-incendios
-forestales-en-galicia-se-repiten-ano-tras-ano/

Epilogue

World Health Organization. WHO Coronavirus (COVID-19)
Dashboard. covid19.who.int/

Index